THE
SPANISH VERB

THE SPANISH VERB

Its forms and uses

TIM CONNELL
Ealing College of Higher Education
and
ELIZABETH VAN HEUSDEN
School of Economics, Utrecht

Stanley Thornes (Publishers) Ltd

First published in 1980 by Stanley Thornes (Publishers) Ltd,
Educa House, Liddington Estate, Leckhampton Road, Cheltenham, Glos, GL53 0DN

British Library Cataloguing in Publication Data

Connell, Timothy
  The Spanish verb.
  I. Spanish language – Verb
  I. Title
  II. Heusden, Elizabeth van.
  Spaanse werkwoord. *Adaptations*
  465   PC4271

ISBN 0 85950 452 2

Typeset by Quadraset Limited, Radstock, Bath, Avon
Printed in Great Britain by The Pitman Press, Bath

Contents

Preface

For many students the Spanish verb, with all its variety of endings, is a major obstacle that prevents them from understanding a particular text or translation. The fact that everything is so different from English hardly helps! This manual is designed to help you see how the system works in Spanish and why the endings change when they do. It lists all the parts of the regular verb and draws attention to the various exceptions to the rule. In addition it explains the various functions of the verb in Spanish and such common stumbling blocks as *ser* and *estar*.

These points are explained as simply and clearly as possible, using plenty of examples, and giving ample explanations. To make sure these are fully understood, a list of terms, in Spanish and English, appears on p. 1.

The Spanish Verb can be used either for learning or revising a particular point, or for quickly checking an irregular form or special usage. To speed the process up, there are four indexes: apart from an alphabetical list of all verbs and words used in the examples, verbs are listed under their various irregular forms; there is a checklist of verbs which are followed by certain prepositions; there is also an index of endings to help you identify and locate the different tenses.

TIM CONNELL
ELIZABETH VAN HEUSDEN

Acknowledgements

Thanks are due to Manuel Fernández-Gasalla and Pilar Connell for their careful reading of the manuscript and their many helpful comments.

This book is a re-modelled version of a book originally published in Holland by Educaboek Stam/Robijns, Culemborg, under the title *Het Spaanse Werkwoord*.

1 Terminology

Whatever you learn – cordon bleu cuisine, car maintenance or a foreign language – you will find that a special range of terms have grown up to help people make themselves understood as simply and accurately as possible. Sometimes you might think that you cannot understand a topic, or you may understand a bit but not know how to frame the questions you want to ask; and that is where understanding the jargon comes in. You may wonder whether Spanish grammar is like anything you have seen in English; or you may not even have studied any English grammar. This book will let you see *how* verbs operate in Spanish; but if you want to know *why* they work as they do, you must be able to follow some of the terminology at least.

ENGLISH TERM	MEANING	SPANISH TERM
personal form	A form of the verb with a Subject e.g. *él toma* – he takes	**forma personal**
impersonal form	A form of the verb with no Subject e.g. *tomando* – taking	**forma impersonal**
simple form	A part of the verb made up of one word e.g. *tomaron* – they took	**forma simple**
compound form	A part made up of two words e.g. *he tomado* – I have taken	**forma compuesta**
gerund	Verbal noun (see p. 37); adds meaning to main verb; *salió cantando* – he went out singing;used to form the present continuous (see p. 20) and verbal phrases (see p. 35).	**gerundio**
infinitive	Expresses meaning without indicating person, tense or number; the basic form of the verb – *tomar, comer, partir* (see p. 30)	**infinitivo**

1

imperative	Verb form used to give commands e.g. *comed* – eat! (See p. 28.)	**modo imperativo**
indicative	Used in relation to fact e.g. *toma el tren* – he takes the train	**modo indicativo**
subjunctive	(see p. 20) Used to suggest implication, possibility or personal attitude; contrast to the Indicative; the form used for parts of the Imperative	**modo subjuntivo**
number	Singular or plural	**número**
past participle	Part of verb used in compound forms e.g. *he tomado;* has descriptive value (see p. 40)	**participio pasado**
person	who is involved	**persona**
reflexive verb	Indicates an action involving the person or thing who is the subject of the verb e.g. *se levanta* – he gets up; also indicates reciprocal action in plural forms (see p. 42)	**verbo reflexivo**
tense	When in time	**tiempo**
auxiliary verb	Verbs, mainly *haber* and *ser,* used to form tenses of other verbs e.g. *ha tomado* – he has taken; *fue matado* – he was killed (see p. 14)	**verbo auxiliar**
defective verb	A verb with only a limited number of forms (see p. 47)	**verbo defectivo**
active	When the subject of the verb is responsible for the action e.g. *el soldado le mató* – the soldier killed him	**voz activa**

2

passive	Shifts emphasis away from the person responsible to the act itself e.g. *fue matado* – he was killed.	**voz pasiva**

All the tenses and moods used in Spanish are identified below, using *tomar* as the example. The parallel equivalent in English is given on the left:

SIMPLE IMPERSONAL FORMS	*FORMAS SIMPLES Y NO PERSONALES*
Infinitive: *to take*	Infinitivo: **tomar**
Gerund: *taking*	Gerundio: **tomando**
Participle: *taken*	Participio: **tomado**

——————— INDICATIVE MOOD ——————— MODO INDICATIVO ———————

SIMPLE PERSONAL TENSES	*TIEMPOS SIMPLES Y PERSONALES*
Present: *I take*	Presente: **tomo**
Imperfect: *I was taking, I used to take*	Imperfecto: **tomaba**
Past Definite: *I took, I did take*	Pretérito: **tomé**
Future: *I shall take*	Futuro: **tomaré**
Conditional: *I would take*	Condicional: **tomaría** (sometimes called the **potencial**)

IMPERSONAL COMPOUND FORMS	*FORMAS COMPUESTAS IMPERSONALES*
Infinitive: *to have taken*	Infinitivo: **haber tomado**
Gerund: *having taken*	Gerundio: **habiendo tomado**

PERSONAL COMPOUND TENSES	*TIEMPOS COMPUESTOS PERSONALES*
Perfect: *I have taken*	Pretérito perfecto compuesto: **he tomado**
Pluperfect: *I had taken*	Pretérito pluscuamperfecto: **había tomado**
Past Anterior: *I had taken*	Pretérito anterior: **hube tomado**

3

Future Perfect:	*I shall have taken*	Futuro perfecto:	**habré tomado**
Conditional Perfect:	*I would have taken*	Condicional perfecto:	**habría tomado**

———————— SUBJUNCTIVE MOOD ———————— MODO SUBJUNTIVO————————

SIMPLE PERSONAL TENSES		*TIEMPOS SIMPLES PERSONALES*	
Present:	*take*	Presente:	**tome**
Imperfect:	*would have taken*	Pretérito imperfecto:	**tomara, tomase**
PERSONAL COMPOUND TENSES		*TIEMPOS COMPUESTOS PERSONALES*	
Present perfect:	*have taken*	Pretérito perfecto:	**haya tomado**
Pluperfect Subjunctive:	*had taken*	Pretérito pluscuamperfecto:	**hubiera, hubiese tomado**

———————— IMPERATIVE MOOD ———————— MODO IMPERATIVO————————

Present:	*take* (singular)	Presente:	**toma**
	take (plural)		**tomad**

(The other forms are supplied by the Subjunctive. See p. 20.)

The thought of learning to recognise all these forms must seem daunting. Luckily most verbs follow a rigid pattern, and although there are irregular forms they tend to follow predictable paths too. But without any doubt you must be able to recognise all the information given by the one or two words that make up the verb. Spanish verbs are extremely concise: they are made up of two elements, the *stem* and the *ending* (sometimes known as the *lexeme* and *morpheme*), one indicating meaning and the other grammatical function. The simple form can tell you in one word time, mood, number, person and voice (or to put it more simply: what is happening, when and who is involved). They are capable of expressing delicate shades of meaning, and a problem for the foreign student lies in the fact that a single letter, even a single *accent*, can change meanings completely:

tomo	*I take*	**tome**	*take!* (imperative)
tomó	*he took*	**tomé**	*I took*

4

And some forms are identical:

tomamos *we take,* or   **tomase** *that I should take,* or
            we took   *that he should take*

So it is essential for you to be able to recognise all the signs immediately. The context is always a useful guide, too.

Do try to be flexible when translating. There is not necessarily an exact single equivalent on a one-to-one basis, and Spanish may use a different tense from English in a particular situation:

llevo un mes aquí *I've been here for a year.*   (See pp. 9, 12.)

The different parts of each tense are always written out in the following order:

SINGULAR

1st person	*I take*	**yo tomo**	
2nd person	*you take*	**tú tomas**	
3rd person	*he/she/it takes*	**él/ella/toma**	(usted: see below)

PLURAL

1st person	*we take*	**nosotros tomamos**	
2nd person	*you take*	**vosotros tomáis**	
3rd person	*they take*	**ellos/ellas toman**	(ustedes: see below)

As the verb ending indicates exactly who is being referred to, it is not necessary to use the personal pronoun all the time:

toman el tren *they're taking the train*

If **it** is the subject, Spanish uses **él** or **ella** when referring to a noun, and if the grammatical gender of the subject is indeterminate, **ello** may be used.

The polite, or formal, style of address is **usted**, usually abbreviated to **Vd.** or **Ud.** (**ustedes, Vds., Uds.** in the plural.) It is used with the third person form of the verb, and although this may sound confusing, there is rarely any doubt in practice as to who is being referred to, because of the context, or other circumstances.

Remember that **tú** and **vosotros** in Spanish are the familiar forms of address, only used for people you consider close to you, as equals – or as inferiors! It is also used when talking to pets or children.

2 Latin American Usages

1) **Vosotros:** this form does not normally appear – except in Church sermons! The plural of **tú** is **ustedes**, a use which sometimes strikes Spaniards as over-formal.

2) **Usted** may be used with children to express parental displeasure; however, in Colombia particularly, and on occasion in other South American countries, it is the common form used between parents and children, and between husband and wife, and may in fact indicate affection rather than annoyance.

Don as a form of address is rather jocular for Latin Americans, although a useful way of indicating courteous familiarity – with one's boss, for instance – in Spain. The Spanish custom of addressing a letter to **Sr. Don** is not typical in Spanish America. But one rather nice usage is **doña, doñita** in Venezuela and Colombia; perhaps a little quaint nowadays, but still in use to imply affection or respect. And unlike **Don** it is not used with the person's name:

Gracias, Don Manolo.   Gracias doñita.

3) **Voseo:** this is a survival from the Spanish of the Conquistadors, and is often found in areas such as Central America, Chile and the countries around the River Plate – Argentina, Uruguay and Paraguay. It is a familiar way of talking to an individual, in place of **tú**. Although teachers will use **tú** in school, and teach it as part of grammar, the **voseo** is its natural replacement at most levels of Society, and in most situations. Notice the stress on the last syllable:

Indicative:	vos **tomás**	vos **comés**	vos **partís**
Subjunctive:	que vos **tomés**	que vos **comás**	que vos **partás**
Imperative:	**tomá** vos	**comé** vos	**partí** vos

The link with **tú** is still there, none the less: **te** is used with reflexives – **ándate vos**; **tu** and **tuyo** are used, although it is possible to say **para vos** and **con vos** instead of **contigo** and **para ti**. The plural of **vos** is **ustedes**.

4) **The Imperative** is often expressed more gently by the Indicative (see p. 29) and the use of **poder** in this situation is not common in the Peninsula (i.e. Spain):

¿Me puedes ayudar?

5) **Past tenses:** where English and Peninsular Spanish use the Perfect tense, in both

6

English and Spanish-speaking America, the Preterite is more likely:

Gracias, ya he comido.   Gracias, ya comí.

6) **-ara/-iera:** these Past Subjunctive endings may be used in place of the Pluperfect Indicative:

cuando llegara = cuando había llegado

cuando comiera = cuando había comido

You may come across examples in Spanish literature or the Press, but it is still occasionally used in Latin America in the spoken language.

7) **Hay/había:** the Imperfect form of **hay** is normally **había**, for both singular and plural. It is not uncommon in Latin America, however, to hear **habían** which, strictly speaking, is an over-correction.

8) **Loísmo:** it is quite common to hear **lo, la** instead of **le** when the person referred to is still grammatically the Direct Object:

lo voy a ver mañana   la llamé por teléfono

9) **Reflexive verbs:** used more widely in Latin America, especially with intransitive verbs:

desayunarse   tardarse   demorarse   recordarse

10) **-le:** something which often confuses the newcomer in countries like Mexico is the habit of adding -le onto the end of an Imperative, for the sake of emphasis—¡córrele! *Run!* And it appears in exclamations like ¡Epale! ¡Híjole!, greetings like ¿Qué hubole? and ándele, meaning *well, there you are then.* However it should be noted that although very common, it is highly colloquial.

3 Uses and Formation of Tenses and Moods

A. SIMPLE FORMS (TIEMPOS SIMPLES)
The Regular Verb

	tomar	comer	partir

Present Tense (Tiempo Presente)

SINGULAR

I take/eat/leave	tomo	como	parto	yo
you	tomas	comes	partes	tú
he/she/it/you	toma	come	parte	él/ella/usted

PLURAL

we take/eat/leave	tomamos	comemos	partimos	nosotros
you	tomáis	coméis	partís	vosotros
they, you	toman	comen	parten	ellos/ellas/ustedes

1) The Spanish verb in this tense may be translated in three different ways in English, depending on the context:

tomo	*I take; I do take; I am taking*
como	*I eat; I do eat; I am eating*
parto	*I leave; I do leave; I am leaving*

NB: the last of these forms does have a direct equivalent in Spanish as well. See p. 20 for the use of the Present Continuous.

2) Some uses are comparable to English:

(a) To describe an existing state or action:

Fernández **vive** en Madrid.   *Fernández lives in Madrid.*
El Talgo **sale** todos los días a las 8.   *The Talgo leaves every day at 8.*

(b) For statements of fact:

Dos y dos **son** cuatro cuatro y dos **son** seis seis y dos **son** ocho y ocho dieciséis.	*Two and two are four . . .* (children's rhyme)

(c) To give orders in a firm, polite way:

Vas al hotel, **hablas** con la recepcionista, y **dices** que llegamos mañana.	*Go to the hotel, speak to reception,* *and say we'll be arriving tomorrow.*

3) It may be used where English uses the Future Tense:

(a) For events in the near future:

El Señor Presidente **sale** mañana.	*The President will leave tomorrow.*

(b) As a question to seek permission or confirmation:

Entonces, nosotros **compramos** el vino, y ustedes la comida, ¿no?	*So, we buy the drink, and you get the* *food, OK?*

4) Where English is more likely to use the Past Tense:

(a) When referring to something in the Present, which has already begun, but not yet ended. This occurs idiomatically with the verbs **llevar** and **hacer**:

Llevo dos meses en Santiago. **Hace** cinco años que trabaja allí.	*I've been in Santiago for two months.* *He's been working there for five* *years.*

(See also p. 12.)

(b) With the Historic Present, particularly in narrative, or story telling. It brings events to life by making them more immediate:

En 1492, los Reyes Católicos **toman** Granada, **expulsan** a los judíos y Colón **descubre** América.	*In 1492 the Catholic Kings took* *Granada, expelled the Jews, and* *Columbus discovered America.*

The Preterite (Pretérito)

SINGULAR

I took/eat/left	tomé	comí	partí	**yo**
you	tomaste	comiste	partiste	**tú**
he/she/it/you	tomó	comió	partió	**él/ella/usted**

9

we	tomamos	comimos	partimos	**nosotros (-as)**
you	tomasteis	comisteis	partisteis	**vosotros (-as)**
they, you	tomaron	comieron	partieron	**ellos/ellas/ustedes**

1) The Preterite corresponds to the simple past in English; the length of time is unimportant – what counts is whether or not it has come to an end:

Esperé cinco minutos.　　　　　*I waited five minutes.*

La ocupación musulmana de　　　*The Moorish occupation of Spain*
España **duró** siete siglos.　　　　*lasted seven centuries.*

2) It also refers to single complete actions:

Fuimos al cine, **vimos** una película　*We went to the pictures, saw a really*
muy buena, **tomamos** una cerveza　*good film, had a beer and then went*
y luego **volvimos** a casa.　　　　*home.*

Note: some verbs are translated differently in the Preterite:

conocer *(to know):*　**Le conocí por primera vez en**　*I first met him in*
　　　　　　　　　　Tenerife.　　　　　　　　　*Tenerife.*

querer *(to want):*　　**Quise verte.**　　　　　　　*I meant to see you.*

saber *(to know):*　　 **Supe de que se trataba.**　　*I found out what it was*
　　　　　　　　　　　　　　　　　　　　　　　　all about.

Imperfect (Imperfecto)

SINGULAR

I was taking/eating/leaving (I used to . . .)	tomaba	comía	partía	**yo**
you	tomabas	comías	partías	**tú**
he/she/it/you	tomaba	comía	partía	**él/ella/usted**

PLURAL

we	tomábamos	comíamos	partíamos	**nosotros(-as)**
you	tomabais	comíais	partíais	**vosotros(-as)**
they/you	tomaban	comían	partían	**ellos/ellas/ustedes**

1) The Imperfect generally indicates continuity. It can be used for an action, characteristic or attitude as they once were:

Cuando yo **era** niño, **pensaba** que
la luna era de queso.

*When I was little, I thought the moon
was made of cheese.*

Mis abuelos siempre **tomaban** el té
a las cinco de la tarde.

*My grandparents always had tea at
five.*

2) Neither start nor finish are relevant, and the contrast with the Preterite in this respect may be seen here:

Yo **salía** de la oficina justo cuando
me llamaste.

*I was leaving the office just as you
rang.*

It can also refer to parallel events:

Los Aztecas **eran** poderosos en
México cuando los Incas **eran**
dueños del Perú.

*The Aztecs were powerful in Mexico
when the Incas were lords of Peru.*

3) In indirect statements and questions, the Imperfect corresponds to the Present Tense in direct ones:

DIRECT

Ricardo dice: **voy** a Caracas.

Richard says: I'm going *to Caracas.*

¿**Empieza** mañana la exposición?

Does *the exhibition start tomorrow?*

INDIRECT

Ricardo dijo que **iba** a Caracas.

Richard said he was going *to Caracas.*

Preguntó si **empezaba** mañana la
exposición.

He asked whether the exhibition
would begin *the next day.*

4) Stylistically the Imperfect may replace either the Preterite or the Conditional to create a more vivid effect, or for impact, but this is rather unusual. More common is the use of the Imperfect instead of the Present Tense in polite phrases:

¿Qué **deseaba**?   *May I help you?* (e.g. in a shop)

¿Qué me **decías**?   *I beg your pardon?*

5) Curiously enough the Imperfect is used to tell the time:

Eran las tres en punto. *It was three on the dot.*

6) **Llevar** and **hacer** (see p. 9) are used in the Imperfect when referring to past time. Note the English equivalents:

Llevaba dos meses en Santiago. *He had been in Santiago for two months.*

Hacía cino años que trabajaba allí. *He had been working there for five years.*

Future (Tiempo Futuro)

SINGULAR

I shall take/eat/leave	tomaré	comeré	partiré	**yo**
you will	tomarás	comerás	partirás	**tú**
he/she/it/you	tomará	comerá	partirá	**él/ella/usted**

PLURAL

we	tomaremos	comeremos	partiremos	**nosotros (-as)**
you	tomaréis	comeréis	partiréis	**vosotros (-as)**
they/you	tomarán	comerán	partirán	**ellos/ellas/ustedes**

The Future Tense does not just refer to things in the Future, as you might expect:

1) In legal language it implies obligation:

Artículo 44: (1) Los poderes públicos **promoverán** y **tutelarán** el acceso a la cultura, a la que todos tienen derecho. *Article 44: (1) of the Constitution: The Public Authorities will promote and supervise access to culture, to which everyone is entitled.*

2) It can express nuances of conjecture and surprise:

¿**Estará** en una reunión su jefe? *Is your boss in a meeting, perhaps?*

¡*Imposible!* No **podrá** negarlo. *Impossible! He can't deny it.*

3) The Indicative is used to indicate future time, if it is in connection with something habitual:

Cuando **va** a Madrid siempre visita el Prado.

When he goes to Madrid he always visits the Prado.

But you use the Subjunctive when referring to a likely future occasion:

Cuando **vayas** a Madrid, visita el Prado.

When you go to Madrid, visit the Prado.

(See p. 20 for further details of the Subjunctive.)

4) An alternative way of expressing the Future is **ir a** + infinitive:

Voy a ver la película mañana.

I'm going to see the film tomorrow.

CHANGING TENSE TO SOFTEN EXPRESSION

The Future and the Conditional, the Future Perfect and Conditional Perfect all refer to things which are yet to come, or which possibly only may come. And so you will find that they may be used to reduce the force behind what you say, to express possibility or merely doubt. They can have the effect then of toning down particular tenses, without being openly negative or contradictory:

Present	→	*Future*
Imperfect	→	*Conditional*
Perfect	→	*Future Perfect*
Pluperfect	→	*Conditional Perfect*

Las carpetas **estarán** en el despacho de usted, ¿no?

The files are in your office – aren't they?

Habría mandado esa carta, porque era urgente.

He must have sent that letter, because it was urgent.

The Conditional (Condicional)

SINGULAR

I would take/eat/leave	tomaría	comería	partiría	**yo**
you	tomarías	comerías	partirías	**tú**
he/she/it/you	tomaría	comería	partiría	**él/ella/usted**

13

we	tomaríamos comeríamos partiríamos	nosotros (-as)
you	tomaríais comeríais partiríais	vosotros (-as)
they/you	tomarían comerían partirían	ellos/ellas/ustedes

1) As the name implies, the Conditional imposes restraints on an idea or course of action whether they are in the Present or Future, whether they are probable, possible or just unlikely:

España **podría** ingresar a la CEE muy pronto.

Spain could join the EEC very soon.

Aprendería el ruso si tuviera tiempo.

I'd learn Russian if I had time.

2) It may be used to give advice:

Deberías hablar con tus padres, ¿no te parece?

You ought to speak to your parents, don't you think?

3) It makes a question sound more polite:

Perdón, ¿**podría** decirme si éste es el camino para la Plaza de España?

Excuse me, can you tell me if this is the way to the Plaza de España?

Note: **quisiera** is generally preferred to **querría**:

Quisiera hablar con el gerente, ahora mismo.

I want to speak to the manager straightaway.

4) In indirect speech it indicates future time:

Emilia dice: **vendré** en seguida.

Emilia says: I'll come immediately.

Emilia dijo que **vendría** en seguida.

Emilia said she would come immediately.

5) It expresses conjecture:

Llegarían al hotel antes de las cinco, ¿no?

They'd arrive at the hotel at about five, wouldn't they?

B. COMPOUND FORMS (TIEMPOS COMPUESTOS)

The Auxiliary Verbs (Verbos auxiliares)

For the complete conjugation of **haber** see p. 65; for **ser** see p. 71; and for **estar** see p. 65.

1) Although **haber** means *to have* it has long since lost any meaning of possession – for that you need to use **tener**. **Haber** is used to create a whole range of compound tenses, so called because two parts are needed for complete understanding; **haber** has the grammatical rôle of expressing tense, number, person and mood, and the past participle used with it (**tomado, comido, partido**) provides the verbal meaning.

2) **Haber** used on its own in the 3rd person singular means *there is, there are;* it is always used in the singular, although in speech (particularly in Latin America) the plural form may be heard:

Hay dos motivos posibles que explican su conducta.	*There are two possible motives to explain his behaviour.*
Había dos motivos posibles que explicaban su conducta.	*There were two motives . . .*

3) Note that an adverb is rarely placed after the Auxiliary, as it is in English:

Siempre lo he dicho.　　　　*I've always said so.*

4) **Ser** is used as the auxiliary to form the Passive voice (see p. 40).

5) **Estar** is used with the Gerund to form the Present Continuous (see p. 20).

6) A wide range of verbs can be used as auxiliaries to add an extra dimension of meaning (see p. 35).

Perfect (Pretérito Perfecto)

SINGULAR

I have taken/eaten/left	he tomado	he comido	he partido	**yo**
you	has tomado	has comido	has partido	**tú**
he/she/it/you	ha tomado	ha comido	ha partido	**él/ella/usted**

PLURAL

we	hemos tomado	hemos comido	hemos partido	**nosotros (-as)**
you	habéis tomado	habéis comido	habéis partido	**vosotros (-as)**
they/you	han tomado	han comido	han partido	**ellos/ellas/ ustedes**

The Perfect Tense forms a link between past and present. It is used in the following circumstances:

1) When the matter referred to lies in the past, but still has some bearing on the present:

> La cuestión de Gibraltar **ha causado** bastante discordia entre los gobiernos de España y la Gran Bretaña.
>
> *The Gibraltar question has caused quite a lot of hard feelings between the UK and Spanish Governments.*

2) When referring to events in the recent past:

> El Primer Ministro **ha pronunciado** un discurso muy importante al respecto.
>
> *The Prime Minister has made a very important speech on the matter.*

And the Perfect may refer to something which has been repeated more than once and may even happen again:

> – ¿Es ésta su primera visita a Lima?
>
> *Is this your first visit to Lima?*

> – No, **he estado** aquí dos veces antes.
>
> *No, I've been here twice before.*

3) To describe the present result of past actions:

> Buñuel **ha dirigido** muchas películas. *Buñuel has directed a lot of films.*

Note: Latin American usage tends to prefer the Preterite in such situations (see p. 6).

Pluperfect (Pretérito Pluscuamperfecto)

SINGULAR

I had taken/eaten/left	había tomado	había comido	había partido	yo
you	habías tomado	habías comido	habías partido	tú
he/she/it/you	había tomado	había comido	había partido	él/ella/usted

16

we	habíamos tomado	habíamos comido	habíamos partido	nosotros(-as)
you	habíais tomado	habíais comido	habíais partido	vosotros(-as)
they/you	habían tomado	habían comido	habían partido	ellos/ellas/ ustedes

1)   The Pluperfect refers to the slightly more remote past; it may link two separate points, going back beyond the one already established:

Cuando llegamos, Pilar y Juliana
habían salido ya.

When we arrived, Pilar and Juliana
had already gone out.

2)   There is a technique of using the Past Subjunctive, ending in -ara, -iera (see p. 19) to indicate the Pluperfect Indicative. It is rather archaic, though, and should be recognised rather than used. Literary examples may be found, it occurs sometimes in the Press, and is still used on occasion in some Latin American Countries.

THE PAST ANTERIOR   *PRETÉRITO ANTERIOR*

You may come across examples of the Past Anterior, which refers to one past action immediately prior to another. It is formed by the Past Participle, preceded by **hube, hubiste, hubo, hubimos, hubisteis, hubieron.** It can usually be spotted by the adverb of Time preceding it, such as: **apenas, aun no, después que, en cuanto, en seguida que, luego que, no bien.**

Apenas hube llamado,
contestaron.

I had hardly called before they
answered.

Note. The Preterite is more commonly used:

En cuanto **llegó**, tomó el
desayuno.

As soon as he arrived, he had
breakfast.

This construction may be found in more formal writing, in the Press for example, in oratory, but not in everyday speech. There is also a similar construction:

Llamado que hube, contestaron.   *As soon as I called, they answered.*

However this is a purely literary construction, found in places such as nineteenth century novels, or literary parodies, and should be recognised rather than used.

Future Perfect (Futuro Perfecto)

SINGULAR

I shall have taken/ eaten/left	habré tomado	habré comido	habré partido	yo
you	habrás tomado	habrás comido	habrás partido	tú
he/she/it/you	habrá tomado	habrá comido	habrá partido	él/ella/usted

PLURAL

we	habremos tomado	habremos comido	habremos partido	nosotros (-as)
you	habréis tomado	habréis comido	habréis partido	vosotros (-as)
they/you	habrán tomado	habrán comido	habrán partido	ellos/ellas/ustedes

1) This Tense looks ahead and tries to establish not just what is going to happen next, but can actually link two events in the future, rather in the way that the Pluperfect (see p. 16) establishes a relationship between two separate points in the past:

El Gobierno **habrá reafirmado** su posición por medio de las próximas elecciones.

The Government will have reconfirmed its position with the coming elections.

2) It can be used in a number of rather subtle ways of making suggestions or guesses:

¿Verdad que los militares **habrán pensado** en intervenir políticamente?

Is it really true that the military have been thinking of intervening politically?

3) You can use it to express probability or something in the recent past:

Son las 3:20; El avión **habrá llegado**, ¿no?

It's 3:20. The plane will have arrived by now, won't it?

4) It is a handy construction in arguments or debate:

. . . aunque esta nueva declaración de parte del gobierno **habrá tenido** cierto impacto en la Bolsa, no afectará a la coyuntura económica actual.

. . . although this new announcement by the government will have some impact on the Stock Exchange, it will not affect the present economic situation.

18

Conditional Perfect (Condicional Perfecto)

SINGULAR

I would have taken/ eaten/left	habría tomado	habría comido	habría partido	**yo**
you	habrías tomado	habrías comido	habrías partido	**tú**
he/she/it/you	habría tomado	habría comido	habría partido	**él/ella/usted**

PLURAL

we	habríamos tomado	habríamos comido	habríamos partido	**nosotros (-as)**
you	habríais tomado	habríais comido	habríais partido	**vosotros (-as)**
they/you	habrían tomado	habrían comido	habrían partido	**ellos/ellas/ustedes**

1) Usage here is parallel to that listed earlier in the Imperfect section, except that it refers to the past, while being related to events in the future.

Si se hubieran declarado nuevas elecciones, el gobierno **habría reafirmado** su posición.	*If new elections had been declared, the government would have reconfirmed its position.*

2) It is equally effective in indicating uncertainty about the past:

¿Es verdad que los Conquistadores **habrían pensado** en matar a Moctezuma?	*Is it true that the Conquistadors would have thought of killing Moctezuma?*

3) Its conditional power is also apparent when referring to something which might have been done, had it been possible:

El gobierno norteamericano **habría intervenido** en la crisis, pero no fue posible.	*The US government might have intervened in the crisis, but it wasn't possible.*

Note: The Subjunctive is used extensively in this sort of construction (see p. 26).

Estoy tomando, *I am taking;* **Estoy comiendo,** *I am eating;*
Estoy partiendo, *I am leaving*

The Continuous forms are comparable to the English construction with *to be;* although they are not separate tenses in their own right, they serve a valuable function in conveying a greater sense of immediacy. They may indicate something which is already going on, and are often used as the starting point in narrative:

No pude contestar el teléfono en ese instante, **estaba comiendo.**

I couldn't answer the phone just then – I was eating.

Allí **estábamos** todos **comiendo** en el café, cuando . . .

There we all were eating in the café, when . . .

Remember though that the simple forms of each tense may have the same translation in English:

Estaba tomando una copa de vino.
Tomaba una copa de vino. }

I was having a glass of wine.

C. THE SUBJUNCTIVE (EL SUBJUNTIVO)

The Present Subjunctive takes its stem from the First Person Singular of the Present Indicative, an important point to remember with irregular verbs (see pp. 62 – 79).

The exact English equivalent of each form is not listed, because the translation will vary according to context:

que partan: *that they leave; that they should leave; for them to leave; let them leave.*

Present Tense (Tiempo Presente de Subjuntivo)

SINGULAR	ar	er	ir	
I	tome	coma	parta	**yo**
you	tomes	comas	partas	**tú**
he/she/it/you	tome	coma	parta	**él/ella/usted**

ar in the subjunctive has the er ending
er + ir have the ar ending

we	tomemos	comamos	partamos	nosotros (-as)
you	toméis	comáis	partáis	vosotros (-as)
they/you	tomen	coman	partan	ellos/ellas/ustedes

Imperfect (Imperfecto de Subjuntivo)

The Past Subjunctive has two forms; in practice they are interchangeable. They are both made up from the Third Person Plural of the Preterite.

SINGULAR   *ar*   *er*   *ir*

I	tomara	comiera	partiera	yo
	tomase	comiese	partiese	
you	tomaras	comieras	partieras	tú
	tomases	comieses	partieses	
he/she/it/you	tomara	comiera	partiera	él/ella/usted
	tomase	comiese	partiese	

PLURAL

we	tomáramos	comiéramos	partiéramos	nosotros (-as)
	tomásemos	comiésemos	partiésemos	
you	tomarais	comierais	partierais	vosotros (-as)
	tomaseis	comieseis	partieseis	
they/you	tomaran	comieran	partieran	ellos/ellas/
	tomasen	comiesen	partiesen	ustedes

Perfect (Pretérito Perfecto de Subjuntivo)

SINGULAR

I	haya tomado/comido/partido	yo
you	hayas tomado/comido/partido	tú
he/she/it/you	haya tomado/comido/partido	él/ella/usted

we	háyamos tomado/comido/partido	nosotros (-as)
you	hayáis tomado/comido/partido	vosotros (-as)
they/you	hayan tomado/comido/partido	ellos/ellas/ustedes

Pluperfect Subjunctive (Pluscuamperfecto de Subjuntivo)

SINGULAR

I	hubiera		*hubiese*	tomado/comido/partido	yo
you	hubieras	OR	*hubieses*	tomado/comido/partido	tú
he/she/it/you	hubiera		*hubiese*	tomado/comido/partido	él/ella/usted

PLURAL

we	hubiéramos		*hubiésemos*	tomado/comido/partido	nosotros (-as)
you	hubierais	OR	*hubieseis*	tomado/comido/partido	vosotros (-as)
they/you	hubieran		*hubiesen*	tomado/comido/partido	ellos/ellas/ ustedes

The Future Subjunctive (Futuro de Subjuntivo)

SINGULAR

I	tomare	comiere	partiere	yo
you	tomares	comieres	partieres	tú
he/she/it/you	tomare	comiere	partiere	él/ella/usted

PLURAL

we	tomáremos	comiéremos	partiéremos	nosotros (-as)
you	tomareis	comiereis	partiereis	vosotros (-as)
they/you	tomaren	comieren	partieren	ellos/ellas/ustedes

It is extremely rare nowadays to see this form, except in legal documents:

Artículo 59:(2) Si el Rey **se inhabilitare** para el ejercicio de su autoridad y la imposibilidad **fuere reconocida** por las Cortes Generales, entrará a ejercer inmediatamente la Regencia el Príncipe heredero de la Corona, si **fuere** mayor de edad.

Article 59 (2) of the Constitution: If the King should become incapable of carrying out his duties, and if Parliament recognises this, the Prince who is heir to the throne shall undertake the powers of Regency forthwith, if he is of age.

You may find examples in literature, and survivals in set phrases such as these:

sea como fuere	*come what may*
por donde fueres, haz lo que vieres	*When in Rome . . .* (literally, wherever you may go, do whatever you may see).

In most situations where the Subjunctive Mood is needed, and future time is implied, use the Present Tense forms. The Imperfect would also be correct in a conditional statement, such as the one above.

HOW TO USE THE SUBJUNCTIVE

The Subjunctive is one of the most complex points of Spanish grammar for students to grasp. In many ways it is comparable to French, with the unfortunate exception that in Spanish the Subjunctive is still widely used, even in conversation, and although ways do exist of avoiding it in places, Spanish speakers do not seem inclined to do so! The fact that it appears so frequently shows how subtle a language Spanish can be; rather than concrete fact, the Subjunctive is used in a whole range of situations where feelings, uncertainties and doubts need to be expressed. It enters into the realm of conjecture and implication and can cover whole ranges of possibility and probability, something which enables the writer or translator to render fine shades of meaning, and introduce a high degree of flexibility, delicacy and style.

1) The Subjunctive is used in the following situations:

(a) after verbs expressing feeling or emotion:

Me alegro de que **haya** venido.	*I'm glad he's come.*
Me temo que **haya** muerto.	*I'm afraid he's died.*

(b) after verbs expressing a wish, or preference, when someone else is involved:

– Quiero que Vd **hable** con el jefe, Sánchez.	*I want you to talk to the boss.*
– No, González, prefiero que **hable** Vd con él.	*No, I'd rather you spoke to him.*

23

(c) with a statement of doubt:

No creo que **haya** llegado.   *I don't think he's arrived.*
Dudo que **haya** llamado.   *I doubt whether he's rung.*
Quizás **haya** escrito.   *He may have written (but I don't*
                                                  think so).

(d) following impersonal expressions:

– Oiga, Sánchez, es urgente que usted **entregue** el reportaje mañana.
– Mire usted, González, no conviene que lo **acabe** tan pronto.
– Entonces es necesario que **hable** con el gerente ahora mismo.
– Ay, es imposible que le **vea** ahora. Estoy muy ocupado.
– Qué terrible que el proyecto se **atrase** por su culpa.

Listen Sánchez, you've got to hand in the report tomorrow. It's urgent.
Look here, González, it's just not possible for me to finish it that quickly.
Well, you'll just have to speak to the manager, right away.
Oh, it's impossible for me to see him now. I'm very busy.
It's a disgrace that the project should fall behind just because of you.

Note: It is possible to avoid using the Subjunctive by using the Infinitive instead:

es urgente **entregar** el reportaje mañana
no conviene **acabarlo** tan pronto
es necesario **hablar** con el gerente
es imposible **verle** ahora
qué terrible **atrasar** el proyecto

Notice, particularly in the last example, that the Subjunctive has greater emphasis in that it draws attention to precisely who is involved. For more information about the Impersonal construction see p. 45.

2) The Subjunctive must be used in the following circumstances:

(a) In connection with Time, following words and phrases such as these:

antes (de) que	*before*	**en cuanto**	*as soon as*	**mientras**	*while*
después (de) que	*after*	**hasta que**	*until*	**cuando**	*when*

However, it is only used when the time is indefinite or refers ahead to some point in the future:

Cuando voy a México siempre **visito**   *When I go to Mexico I (always) visit*
el Museo de Antropología.   *the Anthropology Museum.*

Cuando vaya a México **visitaré** el   *When I go to Mexico I shall visit the*
Museo de Antropología.   *Anthropology Museum.*

24

(b)   The Subjunctive also appears after a number of expressions which reflect the idea of uncertainty, possibility and concession underlying the whole idea of the Subjunctive itself:

Conditional: **a menos (de) que** *unless*   **sin que**   *without*
             con tal (de) que *so long as*   **en caso de que** *in case*

Expressing possibility: **acaso**
                      quizá } *perhaps*
                     tal vez
Concessive: **por más que** } *however much*
              por mucho que

Note: **aunque,** *although,* is followed by the Indicative when concerning statements of fact and corresponding to *although* in English:

Aunque no ha vivido nunca en   *Although he's never lived in Spain he*
España **habla** muy bien español.   *speaks Spanish very well.*

Where it means *even though* or *despite the fact that,* you use the Subjunctive.

Aunque haya vivido muchos años en   *Although he's lived in Spain for*
España habla muy poco español.   *years, he speaks very little Spanish.*

A useful construction for making concessive statements is **por** + **adjective** + **que**:

Por bueno **que** sea González.   *However good Gonzalez may be.*

Por difícil **que** sea esta tarea.   *However hard this job may be.*

(c)   In adjectival clauses related to indefinite or negative points, the Subjunctive must also be used:

Busco una secretaria que **sea** práctica   *I'm looking for a secretary who'll be*
y eficiente.   *practical and efficient.*

No hay nadie que **entienda** este   *There's no-one who can (possibly)*
texto.   *understand this text.*

And there are also these useful constructions:

cualquiera que **sea**   *whichever it might be*
dondequiera que **sea**   *wherever it might be*
quienquiera que **sea**   *whoever he might be*

(d)   The Optative Subjunctive provides what is probably the best known expression in Spanish:

¡**Viva** el Presidente!   *Long live the President!*

¡**Viva** Zapata!   *Up with Zapata!*

25

Or alternatively:

¡Muera el General! *Death to the General!*

It tends to appear in set phrases, often of a pious nature:

Mi abuelo, que en paz descanse. *My grandfather, may he rest in peace.*

Mi tía, que santa gloria haya . . . *My aunty, God rest her soul.*

Dios me libre de esta tarea . . . *Lord, I wish this job was finished . . .*

Ojalá, one of the many legacies of Arabic in Spanish, also takes the Subjunctive:

¡Ojalá que llegue pronto! *Let's hope he gets here soon.*

Sí, ojalá. *Yes, let's hope so.*

3) The Subjunctive is used when speaking of what might have been had something else not happened to prevent it. Spanish allows a whole range of alternatives for both parts of the construction. Indicative forms of the Conditional may appear, besides both forms of the Imperfect Subjunctive:

If this had happened	then	that would have happened
-ara/-iera		-aría/-ería/-iría
-ara/-iera		-ara/-iera
-ara/-iera		-ase/-iese
-ase/-iese		-ara/-iera
-ase/-iese		-aría/-ería/-iría
-aría/-ería/-iría		-ase/-iese

– Oiga, Sánchez, si usted hubiera venido antes, no tendríamos este lío ahora. *Listen, Sanchez, if you'd have come earlier, we wouldn't be having all this trouble now.*

– Mire, González, si usted me hubiera llamado antes por teléfono, yo hubiera llegado a tiempo para la reunión. *Look here, Gonzalez, if you'd have given me a ring, I'd have arrived in time for the meeting.*

– Hombre, si usted comprara un buen reloj, quizá pudiese cumplir con sus compromisos. *Well, if you bought yourself a good watch, perhaps you could keep your appointments.*

– No, señor, eso no es justo. Si la secretaria me hubiese informado de la hora de esta reunión yo no hubiera llegado tarde, ¿eh? *Oh no, that's not fair. If the secretary had told me the time of the meeting I wouldn't have arrived late, would I?*

26

– Pero yo ya le había mandado todos los detalles. Si usted **leyese** toda su correspondencia, no **cometería** tales errores.	*But I'd already sent you all the details. If you read your mail, you wouldn't make mistakes like that.*
– Permítame que le diga una cosa. Yo **leería** todo si usted me **dejase** en paz para leerlo.	*Let me tell you something. I'd read it all if you left me in peace to read it.*

This construction is rather clumsy and complicated. It is hardly surprising that easier everyday alternatives should exist:

– **De haber venido** antes, no tendríamos este lío ahora.	*If you'd have come earlier, we wouldn't be having all this trouble now.*
– **De haberme llamado** por teléfono, yo hubiera llegado a tiempo.	*If you'd have rung me, I would have arrived on time.*
– **De ser** buen administrador, podría obtener buenos resultados.	*If you were a good administrator, you would get good results.*
– **A no ser por** su salud precaria, habría tenido una distinguida carrera.	*Had it not been for his delicate health, he would have had a distinguished career.*

D. THE IMPERATIVE MOOD (EL MODO IMPERATIVO)

1) The Imperative Mood is used to express commands, with the level of formality, urgency or politeness conveyed by tone of voice, context or the choice of expression. The Spanish verb only has two forms which are confined exclusively to giving orders:

2nd person singular:	llama	come	parte	**tú**
2nd person plural:	llamad	comed	partid	**vosotros**

Note: The latter, of course, is not used in Latin America, where the plural of **tú** is **ustedes** (see p. 6).

Do be careful not to confuse the meaning of the **tú** form as it is identical in spelling to the 3rd Person Singular of the Present Indicative:

usted/él/ella:	habla	corre	escribe
you/he/she:	*speaks*	*runs*	*writes*
Imperative:	¡Habla!	¡Corre!	¡Escribe!
	Speak!	*Run!*	*Write!*

A number of verbs have irregular forms in the Imperative:

di	*say*	pon	*put*	sé	*be*	ve	*see*
haz	*do*	sal	*go out*	ten	*have*	ven	*come*

2) Elsewhere (for **nosotros**, **usted**, **ustedes** and negative commands in all tenses) the Subjunctive forms are used (see p. 20).

usted	llame	coma	parta
nosotros	llamemos	comamos	partamos
ustedes	llamen	coman	partan

Negatives:

tú	no llames	no comas	no partas
usted	no llame	no coma	no parta
nosotros	no llamemos	no comamos	no partamos
vosotros	no llaméis	no comáis	no partáis
ustedes	no llamen	no coman	no partan

The use of the Subjunctive indicates the underlying link between wishes and commands. It clearly stresses the distinction between wanting something to be carried out, and having that wish put into effect.

There are various ways of establishing what you want without the force of a direct command:

1) By using the Infinitive:

Para preparar el Pisco Sour	*To make Pisco Sour Cocktail*
Mezclar el limón con la clara de huevo, agregar el Pisco, **licuar** los ingredientes y **servir** con hielo.	*Mix the lemon with the egg white, add the Pisco, blend the ingredients and serve with ice.*

If the Infinitive is used on its own, you should put **a** in front:

Bueno, niños, ¡**a dormir**!	*Right, children, off to bed!*
¡**A comer**!	*Let's eat!*

2) A verb may not even be necessary:

¡Mañana! ¡Aqui! ¡A las ocho!	*Tomorrow! Here! Eight o'clock!*

3) There are all sorts of polite expressions which lack the force of an order, although they suggest that the response should be favourable. Remember, too, that **por favor** is used less in Spanish than *please* in English, as courtesy may be conveyed perfectly adequately by phrases such as these:

¿**Me permite** ver su pasaporte?	*Your passport, please.*
¿**Me podría** dar su nombre?	*Your name, please.*
Haga el favor de abrir esta maleta.	*Open this case, please.*

4) Impersonal constructions may also convey the sense of the Imperative:

Hace falta un permiso de importación para estos artículos.	*An import licence is needed for these articles.*
Es menester llenar un formulario de solicitud.	*An application form has to be filled in.*
Es preciso cumplir con el artículo 123.	*Article 123 has to be obeyed.*
Se prohíbe la entrada a toda persona ajena a esta obra.	*No entry to the site except on business.*

4 The Verb and its Uses

A. THE INFINITIVE (EL INFINITIVO)

tomar	*to take*	comer	*to eat*	partir	*to leave*
haber	*to have left*	haber	*to have eaten*	haber	*to have left*
tomado		comido		partido	

1) Spanish verbs fall into three categories, called conjugations; these are identified by the end letters of the Infinitive form: -ar, -er, -ir. The Infinitive is perhaps the most basic form of the verb. It is the form which appears in dictionaries and word lists, and is given as the starting point for all the other forms. Grammatically, it expresses meaning, without indicating person, tense or number.

2) However it does have various grammatical functions of its own.

(a) As a verbal noun:

Ver es creer.	*Seeing is believing.*
El ir y venir de la gente.	*The coming and going of people.*
El correr es un buen ejercicio.	*Running is good exercise.*

Some verbs have acquired a permanent rôle as nouns:

el deber	*duty*	el pesar	*grief*
el amanecer	*daybreak*	los quehaceres	*jobs to do*

(b) For the Imperative see p. 28.

(c) As a rhetorical exclamation:

¿Yo? ¿Hablar con él?	*What, me? Talk to him?*

(d) After verbs like oír, ver, dejar, mandar, hacer, it may take on a passive value:

Mandar hacer un traje.	*To have a suit made.*
Hemos oído decir que es una compañía muy buena.	*We've heard tell that it is a good company.*

3) A useful range of expressions can be made up with a Preposition:

(a) Al + Infinitive: Time

Al llegar a la estación, me dijeron que había perdido el tren.	*When I arrived at the station, they told me that I'd missed the train.*

Note: The English translation may vary: *on arriving, having arrived.*

(b) Con + Infinitive: Concession

Con **hablar** mucho, no le vas a   *However much you talk you won't*
convencer.   *convince him.*

(c) De + Infinitive: Conditional (see p. 13)

De ser experto en esta materia podría   *If I were an expert on the subject, I*
darle mi opinión.   *could give you my opinion.*

(d) Para + Infinitive: Purpose

Se debe estudiar mucho **para hablar**   *You have to study hard to speak this*
bien este idioma.   *language well.*

Note: **a** is used after **ir** and **venir**:

Viene a comer con nosotros mañana.   *He's coming to eat with us tomorrow.*

Voy a Correos **a** depositar una carta.   *I'm going to the Post Office to post a*
                                            letter.

Note: **Ir a** may also be used to indicate future time (see p. 11).

(e) Por + Infinitive: Cause

Llegó tarde **por haber perdido** el   *He arrived late because he missed the*
tren.   *train.*

4) The Infinitive may appear after adverbs, conjunctions and pronouns; it is often an alternative construction to the Subjunctive:

Te llamará por teléfono después **de**   *He'll give you a ring after dinner*
cenar, y antes de **acostarse.**   *before he goes to bed.*

(Or using the Subjunctive): después de que **cene** y antes de que **se acueste.**

No podemos darle nuestra respuesta   *We cannot give you our answer until*
sin **estudiar** los documentos.   *we've studied the documents.*

(Or using the Subjunctive): sin que **estudiemos** los documentos.

De haber consultado los   *If you'd studied the regulations, you*
reglamentos, no tendría este lío ahora.   *wouldn't have all this trouble now.*

(Or using the Subjunctive): **Si hubiera consultado** los reglamentos . . .
See p. 26 for further examples.

31

1)   When referring to a specific person or a particular animal, such as a pet, **a** is placed after the verb:

Vimos **a** mi hermano anoche.   *We saw my brother last night.*

Sacamos **al** perro a pasear ayer.   *We took the dog out for a walk yesterday.*

2)   With collective nouns, the rule is less certain:

Sí conozco (**a**) la familia.   *Yes, I do know the family.*

3)   It is also used with things personified, or places with special meaning:

Defender **a** la Patria.   *To defend the country.*

Recuerdo con mucho afecto **a** Veracruz.   *I have fond memories of Veracruz.*

4)   However, Personal **a** is not used when the person is unspecified:

Se busca criada.   *Maid wanted.*

Necesito un profesor que pueda ayudarme.   *I need a teacher who can help me.*

Llame un médico, ¡pronto!   *Call a doctor, quickly!*

B.   SER and ESTAR

Spanish has the curious feature of using two different verbs meaning *to be:*

1) **Ser** is used in connection with universal or inherent qualities, or something which is normally thought of as an integral feature, or a permanent individual characteristic. It is also the verb used as part of impersonal expressions (see p. 45) and as the Auxiliary Verb to form the Passive Mood (see p. 40).

2) The choice between **ser** and **estar** is not always clearcut, so the following examples will give some indication of when to use **ser:**

(a)   Qualities and characteristics:

Es una muchacha simpática y muy guapa.   *She's a nice girl, and smart too.*

Este vino **es** de muy buena calidad.   *This is a fine quality wine.*

Este juguete **es** de plástico.   *This toy's made of plastic.*

(b) Nationality:
Ricardo **es** Peruano.   *Richard is Peruvian.*

(c) Origin:
Este vino **es** de Rioja.   *This wine is from Rioja.*

(d) Occupation:
María **es** profesora.   *Mary is a teacher.*

(e) Religion:
Isabel **es** católica.   *Isabel is Catholic.*

(f) Politics:
Este gobierno **es** muy conservador.   *This government is highly conservative.*

(g) Possession:
Este libro **es** mío.   *This book is mine.*

(h) Time:
Son las ocho.   *It's eight o'clock.*

3) **Estar** tends to be less permanent, relating to a transitory state, or a condition which is liable to change. It also indicates the result of a process or past action, and is used especially with a past participle. In addition, it describes location.

(a) State:
El gobierno **estaba** muy inestable en aquella época.   *The government was highly unstable at that time.*

(b) Result of a process:
El reportaje oficial **está** listo.   *The official report is ready.*
Ya **está** terminado el informe anual.   *The annual report is finished.*

(c) Location:
Valencia **está** en España.   *Valencia is in Spain.*

4) Causes of confusion

(a) Inevitably confusions do arise as the logic behind each usage is not always apparent. (For instance, it may seem contradictory to say that **estar** conveys a transitory idea on the one hand, and then use it to describe the location of a city. The reason here is historical – **estar** derives from the Latin **stare,** to stand.)

(b) The meaning of an adjective may change depending on your use of **ser** or **estar:**

Mario **es** vivo.   *Mario is quick-witted.*

Mario **está** vivo.   *Mario is alive.*

Dolores **es** lista.	*Dolores is bright.*
Dolores **está** lista.	*Dolores is ready.*
Angeles **es** alegre.	*Angeles is happy (by nature).*
Angeles **está** alegre.	*Angeles is happy (for the moment).*
Doña Mercedes **es** (una) enferma.	*Doña Mercedes is an invalid.*
Doña Mercedes **está** enferma.	*Doña Mercedes is unwell.*

(c)   The use of **ser** and **estar** with a participle often creates difficulties too. Remember **ser** is used when describing an action:

El soldado **fue** herido por una bala.	*The soldier was wounded by a bullet.*
	(See p. 40 for use of the Passive.)

Estar usually indicates the state resulting from an action, describing the actual situation:

El soldado **está** herido.	*The soldier is wounded.*
	(i.e. he has been hurt).

This distinction also explains otherwise curious usages such as these:

está muerto	*he is dead*
está casado	*he is married* (**casado** here is a participle)
es casado	*ditto* – but **casado** here is a noun

5)   **Estar** takes on a variety of meanings when followed by certain prepositions:

Estar de vacaciones	*to be on holiday*	**estar** de guardia	*to be on guard*
estar de viaje	*to be travelling*	**estar** de luto	*to be in mourning*
estar de prisa	*to be in a hurry*	**estar** de embajador	*to be acting as ambassador*

It may also indicate points in time, with **por** and **para**:

Está por escribir la historia de la Compañía Catalana.	*The story of the Catalan company has yet to be written.*
Estoy para salir.	*I'm just about to go out.*

They may both be used with nouns, too:

Estoy por el teatro.	*I'm in favour of going to the theatre.*
Estoy para una copa de vino.	*I feel like a glass of wine.*

6)   **Estar** is used with the Gerund to form the Present Continuous Tense (see p. 20).

7)   Stylistically a whole range of verbs can be used instead of **ser** and **estar** (see p. 35).

C. VERBAL PHRASES (LAS FRASES VERBALES)

1) It has already been seen how the verb in Spanish provides you with a whole set of information in the most compact way possible, in just one or two words. But a range of phrases exists which, used with the Infinitive, Gerund or Participle, either enriches the style of expression or provides additional information.

2) In some cases, the verb acts as an Auxiliary and can be used in place of **ser** and **estar**:

llevar	quedar(se)	verse
tener	dejar	hallarse

Tengo proyectados varios planes.   *I have various plans lined up.*

Quedan suspendidas las clases.   *Classes are suspended.*

Notice that the Participle agrees with the noun (as you would expect in French).

This does not happen, of course, with **haber** (see p. 14), although it does with the Passive (see p. 40).

3) Other common expressions fall into six categories.

(a) Starting off:

comenzar a	lanzarse a
echar(se) a	pasar a
empezar a	ponerse a
ir a	romper a

} + Infinitive

Se **echaron** a correr.   *They ran off.*

Se **puso** a escribir.   *He began to write.*

(b) Continuing:

andar	seguir
ir	venir

} + Gerund

Sigue pensando que la reunión tendrá lugar mañana.   *He keeps thinking the meeting will be tomorrow.*

Note: **ir a** may be used to form the Future Tense (see p. 11).

Vamos a ver si ha llegado: May be shortened to **A ver si ...**

35

(c) Reiterating:

volver a + Infinitive

Vuelvo a repetir: ¿por qué llega usted siempre tarde?	*I'll ask you again: why do you always arrive late?*

(d) Finishing off:

acabar de
acabar por
}

llegar a
terminar por
} + Infinitive

Acaban de nombrarle Jefe de Ventas.	*They've just made him Head of Sales.*
Acabaron por nombrarle jefe de publicidad.	*They finally appointed him Head of Publicity.*
Terminaron por despedir al ingeniero jefe.	*They ended up by sacking the Chief Engineer.*

(e) Obliging:

deber
tener que
}

haber de
haber que
} + Infinitive

Tendrán que consultarme primero.	*They'll have to consult me first.*
Hay que publicar estos datos cuanto antes.	*These data must be published as soon as possible.*

(f) Supposing:

deber de   venir a

La instalación de esa planta vendrá a costar más de 50 mil.	*Installing that plant is going to cost something well over 50 thousand.*
Debe de haber llegado mi carta.	*My letter should have arrived.*

Note: do not confuse this with **debe haber llegado** – *it must have arrived.*

5 Participles and the Passive

A. THE PRESENT PARTICIPLE (PARTICIPIO PRESENTE)

1) For all practical purposes the Present Participle (-ante, -ente, -iente) fell out of use in Spanish long ago and its place was taken mainly by the Gerund (see below). But it does survive in a few cases.

2) By no means all verbs have a form with this ending, however, and these may appear as adjectives:

ausente	*absent*	fascinante	*fascinating*
conveniente	*convenient*	participante	*participating*
concerniente	*concerning*	permanente	*permanent*
correspondiente	*corresponding*	presente	*present*
recurrente	*recurring*	tocante	*regarding*
sobresaliente	*outstanding*	semejante	*similar*

Be careful with words having these endings, though, because there are also nouns, in a business context, for example:

el inconveniente	*inconvenience*	el representante	*representative*
el equivalente	*equivalent*	el solicitante	*applicant*
el firmante	*signatory*	el sobrante	*surplus*
el querellante	*plaintiff*	la vacante	*vacancy*

They may also be used as adverbs and prepositions:

durante	*during*	no obstante	*none the less*
mediante	*via*	por consiguiente	*consequently*

B. THE GERUND (GERUNDIO)

Simple form:

tomando	*taking*	comiendo	*eating*	partiendo	*leaving*

Compound form:

habiendo tomado	*having taken*	habiendo comido	*having eaten*	habiendo partido	*having left*

1) The simple form indicates a parallel occurrence, and when one action cuts across another:

> Entré en la oficina y vi a la secretaria **escribiendo** a máquina.
>
> *I went into the office and saw the secretary typing.*

The compound form is used in connection with prior events or actions:

> **Habiendo examinado** estas cifras, mi consejo es vender las acciones.
>
> *Having considered these figures, my advice is to sell the shares.*

With the exception of words like **ardiendo, hirviendo,** the Gerund is not used as an adjective. It can, however, operate in the context of a verb or adverb, and so you should be particularly careful not to confuse its rôle when you see it.

2) It is used as part of certain verbal phrases to indicate:

(a) Continuity, and to prolong the action (see p. 35).

(b) Manner:

> Salió **gritando** de la reunión.
>
> *He went storming out of the meeting.*

(c) Means:

> Aproveche esta gran oferta **enviando** un giro postal . . .
>
> *Take advantage of this great offer by sending a postal order . . .*

(d) Cause (or to support an argument):

> No me gusta este proyecto, **empezando** por el estilo y **terminando** con las medidas que propone.
>
> *I don't like this project, beginning with the style, and ending with the measures it proposes.*

(e) Concessive (or with a Conditional value):

> **Participando** todos, la feria de muestras tendrá un gran éxito.
>
> *If everyone takes part, the samples trade fair will be a great success.*

3) It should not be used to express consequence, effects or later actions, but with **en** it can refer to an action which has just taken place:

> **En anunciando** esto, se sentó.
>
> *Having announced this, he sat down.*

This is rather outdated nowadays, however.

4) Pronouns are attached to the end of the Gerund:

tomándo**los**   comiéndo**la**

habiéndo**lo** tomado   habiéndo**lo** comido

Notice the accent, used to denote that the point of stress has not changed.

Alternatively, the pronoun may go first, in front of the Auxiliary:

lo está tomando   **lo** está comiendo

5) The Subject, if mentioned, always follows the Gerund:

Habiéndose retirado **el gerente**, fue reemplazado muy pronto.	*The manager having retired, a replacement was soon found.*

BEWARE OF CONFUSION

You can see that the Gerund in Spanish often corresponds to *-ing* in English; but English usage does differ in a number of ways:

1) *-ing* may be translated by the Past Participle in Spanish:

Un retrato **colgado** en la pared	*A picture* hanging *on the wall*
El conserje, **sentado** a la ventana . . .	*The caretaker,* sitting *at the window . . .*

2) Some English adjectives ending in *-ing* have **-ado/-ido** endings in Spanish:

accommodating	comedido	*trusting*	confiado
daring	atrevido	*audacious*	osado

3) English verbs ending in *-ing* can be a pitfall too:

Those wanting *to enrol . . .*	Los que **deseen** inscribirse . . .
Even taking *into account those customers paying in advance . . .*	Aun **tomando** en cuenta a los clientes que paguen por adelantado . . .

Notice too that although verbs of perception or representation (**oír, ver**) are usually followed by the Gerund, in the situation given here, the Infinitive may be used to suggest a completed action:

Vi al jefe **dictando cartas.**	*I watched the boss dictating letters.*
Vi al jefe **dictar** cartas.	

And be careful when writing letters in Spanish not to imitate English style:

Estimado Don Manuel, **Escribo** esta carta para informarle...	*Dear Manuel, I am writing to let you know . . .*
Distinguido cliente, Por medio de la presente le **comunicamos** que . . .	*Dear Customer, We are sending you this letter to tell you . . .*

C. THE PAST PARTICIPLE (PARTICIPIO PASADO)

tomado *taken*   comido *eaten*   partido *left*

1)   The Participle appears as part of a wide range of different constructions:

(a)   With **haber** to form Compound Tenses (see p. 14).

(b)   With **ser** to form the Passive (see below).

(c)   With another verb in front of it to form a Verbal Phrase (see p. 35).

Note: the Participle is invariable, keeping exactly the same ending, when used with **haber**. It agrees in number and gender with the Subject in (b) and (c) above.

2)   The Participle also has a number of rôles to play in its own right.

(a)   In absolute constructions, which are commoner in Spanish than English:

Time
> **Terminada** la conferencia, me fui.   *When the lecture was over, I left.*

Manner
> **Animados** por el éxito de la huelga, volvieron a trabajar.   *Encouraged by the success of the strike they went back to work.*

Conditional
> **Considerado** desde ese punto de vista, el proyecto es muy razonable.   *Looked at from that point of view, the project is very reasonable.*

(b)   As verbal adjectives with an active meaning:

agradecido	*grateful*	**leído**	*well read*
callado	*quiet*	**parecido**	*similar*
desesperado	*desperate*	**presumido**	*vain*

D. THE PASSIVE (LA VOZ PASIVA)

ser tomado *to be taken*   **ser comido** *to be eaten*   **ser recibido** *to be received*

For the various forms of **ser** see p. 71.

The Past Participle agrees with the Subject:

> El gobierno fue severamente criticado.   *The government was severely criticised.*

> La junta fue severamente criticada.   *The junta was severely criticised.*

> Las secretarias fueron despedidas.   *The secretaries were sacked.*

1) The Passive in Spanish is made up of **ser** and the Past Participle. As a verb form, the Passive has the effect of altering the psychological viewpoint and shifting emphasis *to* the action *from* those responsible:

Active

La compañía pronto entregó las piezas de repuesto.	*The company soon delivered the spare parts.*

Passive

Las piezas de repuesto fueron entregadas pronto por la compañía.	*The spare parts were soon delivered by the company.*

Active

Unos terroristas **asesinaron** ayer al Presidente.	*Terrorists assassinated the President yesterday.*

Passive

El Presidente **fue asesinado** ayer por unos terroristas.	*The President was assassinated yesterday by terrorists.*

2) In practice the tendency is not to use the Passive with the Present or Imperfect tenses, as these would imply continuous rather than completed actions and the dictates of style would therefore require things to be put differently. An important point to remember is that the Passive is used far less in Spanish than in English.

You do not have to go to the extremes of actively avoiding it, but there are preferable alternatives. See p. 42 for the use of **se**.

3) None the less, the Passive is useful to express a degree of uncertainty or to take the edge off what is said:

González no va a solicitar ese nuevo puesto en la compañía.	*Gonzalez isn't going to put in for that new job in the company.*
¿Por qué **ha sido disuadido?**	*Why has he been put off?*
¿No sabía? El contrato con el Perú **fue perdido** por culpa suya.	*Didn't you know? The contract with Peru was lost because of him.*

41

E. THE REFLEXIVE AND *SE*

cortarse *to cut oneself*   **mantenerse** *to maintain oneself*   **servirse** *to help oneself*

yo **me** corto	*yo* **me** mantengo	*yo* **me** sirvo
tú **te** cortas	*tú* **te** mantienes	*tú* **te** sirves
él/ella/usted **se** corta	*él/ella/usted* **se** mantiene	*él/ella/usted* **se** sirve
nosotros **nos** cortamos	*nosotros* **nos** mantenemos	*nosotros* **nos** servimos
vosotros **os** cortáis	*vosotros* **os** mantenéis	*vosotros* **os** servís
ellos/ellas/ustedes **se** cortan	*ellos/ellas/ustedes* **se** mantienen	*ellos/ellas/ustedes* **se** sirven

Note: the same pronouns are used with all the other tenses e.g. **me** *corté*, **se** *mantenía*, **nos** *habíamos servido*, etc.

1)   With Reflexive verbs the Subject and Object are the same person or thing. This means that a particular action relates back to the person responsible for it.

> María **se** despierta a las ocho, **se** levanta, **se** lava y **se** viste.　　*Maria wakes up at eight, gets up, has a wash and gets dressed.*

English may use *himself/herself* with similar effect – *dresses herself*, or *gets herself off to school*. But few English verbs are purely reflexive; *to pride oneself* is probably the only one in normal use today. Spanish, on the other hand, has a large number of verbs which are only reflexive – often where their English equivalents are not.

2)   The use of **se** may indicate that an action is reciprocal – there is a mutual element:

> González y Sánchez **se** gritaban.　　*Gonzalez and Sanchez were shouting at each other.*

> No **nos** conocemos muy bien, pero él me parece muy simpático.　　*We don't know each other very well, but he seems very pleasant to me.*

Ambiguity may arise in certain circumstances:

> **Los soldados se mataron.**　　(a)　*The soldiers killed each other.*
> 　　(b)　*The soldiers killed themselves.*

Various phrases are available to make matters clear:

(a)	el uno al otro	(b)	a él mismo	a nosotros(as) mismos(as)
	mutuamente		a ella misma	a vosotros(as) mismos(as)
	recíprocamente		a sí mismo(a)	a ellos(as) mismos(as)

3) The Reflexive can alter the meaning of a verb. It can emphasise or intensify an action:

Juliana comió la manzana.   *Juliana ate the apple.*

Juliana **se** comió la manzana.   *Juliana ate the whole apple.*

And compare the following:

dormir	*to sleep*	dormirse	*to go to sleep*
esperar	*to wait*	esperarse	*to hang on for a bit*
ir	*to go*	irse	*to go away*
morir	*to die*	morirse	*to be dying*

4) With the Imperative form (see p. 28) the Pronoun is added to the end of the verb:

duérmete *go to sleep*   **váyanse**   *go away*

And there are set phrases: **érase una vez** . . .   *Once upon a time* . . .

5) With the First and Second Person Plural of the Imperative, the last letters are left off when the Pronoun is added:

	nosotros	**vosotros**	
esperarse	esperémonos	esperaos	
detenerse	detengámonos	deteneos	
servirse	sirvámonos	servíos	
irse	vámonos	idos	(Exception to the rule)

6) The Reflexive is commonly used where English would use the Passive:

(a) Personal

Los ejecutivos **se esforzaron** por acabar el informe.   *Every effort was made by the executives to finish the report.*

Las materias primas ya no **se exportan** sin la documentación debida.   *Raw materials are no longer exported without the necessary documents.*

(b) Impersonal

Se espera que su compañía pueda cumplir con lo prometido.   *It is to be hoped that his company can do what was promised.*

Se supone que el gobierno va a proponer nuevas medidas.   *It is to be supposed that the government will propose new measures.*

| Se puede telefonear aquí. | *Phone calls may be made from here.* |
| Se prohíbe la entrada. | *No entry.* |

(For other impersonal constructions, see p. 45.)

7) It is quite common to see a plural verb too, although the grammatical accuracy of this has been the subject of long debate, with the Real Academia deciding against such a usage. It may be a *galicismo,* a result of the influence of *on* in French, or simply a spontaneous development in Spanish; it is rarely found in literary style.

| Se busca informes | } | *Information is being sought* |
| Se buscan informes | | |

Remember that if you want to use a Reflexive verb in this impersonal way, you have to use **uno** instead of **se**:

| Uno se queja siempre del servicio en estos hoteles. | *One always complains about service in these hotels.* |

8) **Uno** is used like the French *on* (though less often):

| Uno trabaja todo el día, y ¿para qué? | *You work all day, and what for?* |

6 Impersonal Verbs

1) Spanish has a whole range of verbs which are used only in impersonal constructions; in this respect, of course, they are unusual rather than irregular! Some are a useful feature of everyday language, like **gustar, hay** or **es que**; others are valuable in more formal contexts:

caber	*to be fitting, to contain*	hacer falta	*to be necessary*
convenir	*to be right*	bastar	*to be enough*
doler	*to regret*	interesar	*to be of interest*
faltar	*to be lacking*	valer	*to be worth*

Falta tiempo para ver todo el mundo.   *Time is needed to see the whole world.*

Cabe mencionar las obras de Dalí.   *The works of Dalí are worth mentioning.*

(a) Some of these expressions are used with **se** (see p. 42):

se estima que	*it is reckoned that*	**se** olvida que	*it is forgotten that*
se entiende que	*it is understood that*	**se** supone que	*it is supposed that*

Se supone que este proyecto requiere cuantiosas inversiones   *It is supposed that this project will require heavy investments.*

(b) **Ser** may be used in a wide range of phrases:

es preciso	*it is essential*	**es** menester	*it is necessary*
es imposible	*it is impossible*	**es** innegable	*it is undeniable*
es imprescindible	*it is unavoidable*	**es** verdad	*it is true*

Es verdad que Sánchez trabaja mucho.   *It is true that Sanchez works hard.*

No es verdad que González sea puntual.   *It's not true that that Gonzalez is punctual.*

2) Set phrases:

(a) With **ser** and **estar:**

es de día	*it's daylight*	está nublado	*it's cloudy*
es tarde	*it's late*	está oscuro	*it's dark*

(b) With **hacer**

Hace frío	*it's cold*	hace sol	*it's sunny*
Hace calor	*it's hot*	hace buen tiempo	*it's nice weather*

And, of course, **hacer** is used with expressions of Time:

Hace dos horas que está nevando.   *It's been snowing for two hours.*

Hace dos horas que llegó.
Llegó **hace** dos horas.   *He arrived two hours ago.*

HACE

Notice the Tense changes between the two languages:

ENGLISH		SPANISH
Pluperfect	:	Imperfect
Future Perfect	:	Future
He had arrived two hours before.		**Hacía dos horas que había llegado.**
I'll have been living here for four years.		**Hará cuatro años que vivo aquí.**

---

3) The Third Person Plural (*they*) may also be used in Impersonal expressions, just like the English, in fact:

Dicen que será Presidente algún día.   *They say he'll be President one day.*

And **se** may also be used:

Se dice que será Presidente algún día.   *They say he'll be President one day.*

See p. 42 for details.

4) Some verbs are exclusively impersonal in use, and therefore are only used in the Third Person Singular of the Indicative and Subjunctive; the Infinitive, Gerund and Past Participle may also be found. Many of these verbs relate to the natural world:

amanecer	*to dawn*	**llover**	*to rain*
anochecer	*to get dark*	**granizar**	*to hail*
helar	*to freeze*	**nevar**	*to snow*

46

7 Defective Verbs

A number of verbs do not have complete conjugations – only certain forms exist:

concernir *(to concern)*   concierne, conciernen; concernía, concernían; concierna, conciernan;

abolir *(to abolish)*   aboliendo; abolido; abolimos, abolís; abolid; The Preterite (**abolí** etc), Imperfect (**abolía** etc), the Future (**aboliré** etc), the Conditional (**aboliría** etc) and both forms of the Imperfect Subjunctive (**aboliera**, **aboliese** etc) are all used normally.

Note: **agredir** and **transgredir** follow the same pattern.

soler *(to be accustomed)*   Only the Present and Imperfect Indicative (**suelo** etc and **solía** etc) are normally used, although the Present Subjunctive may sometimes appear.

yacer *(to lie)*   Given its use in tombstone inscriptions, it would be rare to see any other than the Third Person forms.

Note also the irregular forms **yazca**, **yazga** and **yaga** in the Present Subjunctive.

47

8 Radical Changing Verbs

These verbs change slightly in spelling, when stress is placed on the stem, or lexeme, but only with the First, Second and Third Person Singular, and the Third Person Plural: *yo, tú, él/ella/ello/usted* and *ellos/ellas/ustedes*. And this only applies to certain tenses, listed below.

They may be divided into four categories:

---

e > ie

Perder *to lose*

INDICATIVO

Presente   pierdo, pierdes, pierde, perdemos, perdéis, pierden

SUBJUNTIVO   pierda, pierdas, pierda, perdamos, perdáis, pierdan

IMPERATIVO   pierde

Common verbs which follow the same pattern:

acertar	*to be correct*	despertar	*to waken*
alentar	*to encourage*	desterrar	*to exile*
apretar	*to press*	empezar	*to begin*
arrendar	*to rent*	encender	*to light*
ascender	*to promote, raise*	enmendar	*to amend*
asentar	*to settle, found*	entender	*to understand*
atender	*to serve*	enterrar	*to bury*
atravesar	*to cross*	errar	*to err*
calentar	*to heat*	escarmentar	*to get your comeuppance*
cegar	*to blind*	extender	*to extend*
cerrar	*to close*	fregar	*to rub*
comenzar	*to begin*	gobernar	*to govern*
concertar	*to agree*	helar	*to freeze*
confesar	*to confess*	manifestar	*to demonstrate*
defender	*to defend*	merendar	*to have tea*
descender	*to fall*	negar	*to deny*

48

nevar	*to snow*	sembrar	*to sow*
pensar	*to think*	sentarse	*to sit down*
perder	*to lose*	temblar	*to tremble*
quebrar	*to break*	tender	*to stretch*
recomendar	*to recommend*	tentar	*to try*
regar	*to irrigate*	tropezar	*to stumble*
segar	*to mow*	tropezar con	*to come across (someone)*
		verter	*to pour*

There is no simple rule to remember which verbs change and which do not. But a useful guide is the noun which corresponds to the verb:

asentar	el asentamiento	*settlement*
comenzar	el comienzo	*beginning*
desterrar	el destierro	*exile*
enmendar	la enmienda	*amendment*
enterrar	el entierro	*burial*
gobernar	el gobierno	*government*
nevar	la nieve	*snow*
quebrar	la quiebra	*break, bankruptcy*
regar	el sistema de riego	*irrigation system*

Note: for more on **errar** see p. 77.

Pedir   *to ask for*

Infinitivo	pedir
Gerundio	pidiendo
Participio pasado	pedido

INDICATIVO

Presente	pido, pides, pide, pedimos, pedís, piden
Pretérito	pedí, pediste, pidió, pedimos, pedisteis, pidieron

SUBJUNTIVO

Presente	pida, pidas, pida, pidamos, pidáis, pidan
Imperfecto	pidiera, pidieras, pidiera, pidiéramos, pidierais, pidieran

IMPERATIVO

tú	pide

Common verbs with the same pattern:

ceñir	*to surround*	impedir	*to prevent*
competir	*to compete*	medir	*to measure*
concebir	*to conceive*	perseguir	*to pursue*
conseguir	*to get*	proseguir	*to carry on with*
corregir	*to correct*	reir	*to laugh*
derretir	*to melt*	sonreír	*to smile*
despedir	*to dismiss*	rendirse	*to surrender, give up*
despedirse	*to say goodbye*	reñir	*to quarrel*
elegir	*to elect*	repetir	*to repeat*
engreír	*to spoil; make conceited*	seguir	*to follow*
freir	*to fry*	servir	*to serve*
gemir	*to groan*	teñir	*to dye*
henchirse	*to swell*	vestir	*to dress*

Note: for more on **reir, sonreír, reñir** and **ceñir, teñir** see pp. 77–79.

Sentir

to feel

Infinitivo	sentir
Gerundio	sintiendo
Participio pasado	sentido

INDICATIVO

Presente	siento, sientes, siente, sentimos, sentís, sienten
Pretérito	sentí, sentiste, sintió, sentimos, sentisteis, sintieron

SUBJUNTIVO

Presente	sienta, sientas, sienta, sintamos, sintáis, sientan
Imperfecto	sintiera, sintieras, sintiera, sintiéramos, sintierais, sintieran
	sintiese, sintieses, sintiese, sintiésemos, sintieseis, sintiesen

IMPERATIVO

tú	siente

Common verbs with the same pattern:

adquirir	*to acquire*	hervir	*to boil*
arrepentirse	*to feel remorse*	mentir	*to lie*
adherirse a	*to stick to*	requerir	*to require*
herir	*to hurt, wound*	sentir	*to regret; feel sorry*

verbs ending in **-vertir**		verbs ending in **-ferir**	
advertir	*to notice*	conferir	*to confer, present*
convertir	*to convert*	diferir	*to differ*
divertirse	*to have fun*	preferir	*to prefer*
invertir	*to invest*	referirse a	*to refer to*
		transferir	*to transfer*

Note: for more on **adquirer, inquirir**, see p. 69; for **erguir**, p. 76.

Mover *to move*

INDICATIVO

Presente   **muevo, mueves, mueve,** movemos, movéis, **mueven**

SUBJUNTIVO

Presente   **mueva, muevas, mueva,** movamos, mováis, **muevan**

IMPERATIVO

tú   **mueve**

Common verbs with the same pattern:

absolver	*to absolve*	forzar	*to force*
acordar	*to agree*	llover	*to rain*
acostarse	*to go to bed*	morder	*to bite*
almorzar	*to have lunch*	mostrar	*to show*
apostar	*to bet*	oler	*to smell*
aprobar	*to approve*	probar	*to try, test*
avergonzarse	*to be ashamed*	recordar,	
cocer	*to cook*	acordarse de	*to remember*
colgar	*to hang up*	renovar	*to renew*
comprobar	*to prove*	rogar	*to request*
consolar	*to console*	soler	*to be used to*
conmover	*to move (emotionally)*	soltar	*to release*
contar	*to count, tell*	sonar	*to sound*
costar	*to cost*	soñar	*to dream*
demostrar	*to show*	torcer	*to twist*
desaprobar	*to disapprove*	volar	*to fly*
devolver	*to give back*	volcar	*to turn over*
doler	*to hurt*	volver	*to return*
encontrar	*to find, meet*		
esforzarse por	*to make an effort*		

NB: **jugar** also follows this pattern. For notes on **avergonzarse** see p. 75.

Useful guide:

almorzar	el almuerzo	*lunch*
apostar	la apuesta	*bet*
contar {	el cuento	*the story*
	la cuenta	*the bill*
forzar	la fuerza	*force*
mostrar	la muestra	*sample*
soñar	el sueño	*dream*
volar	el vuelo	*flight*

Note: for more on **oler**, see p. 77.

Dormir and **morir** not only have the o > ue change listed above, but also change o > u in the Gerund, the Third Person Singular and Plural of the Preterite, and in the Subjunctive:

Dormir   *to sleep*

Infinitivo	dormir
Gerundio	**durmiendo**
Participio pasado	dormido (NB: *morir* is irregular: **muerto**)

INDICATIVO

Presente	**duermo, duermes, duerme,** dormimos, dormís, **duermen**
Pretérito	dormí, dormiste, **durmió,** dormimos, dormisteis, **durmieron**

SUBJUNTIVO

Presente	**duerma, duermas, duerma, durmamos, durmáis, duerman**
Imperfecto	**durmiera, durmieras, durmiera, durmiéramos, durmierais, durmieran**
	durmiese, durmieses, durmiese, durmiésemos, durmieseis, durmiesen

IMPERATIVO

tú	**duerme**

53

9 Other Changes

A. CHANGES IN SPELLING

The Spanish alphabet is virtually phonetic. This means that with some exceptions like *h* each letter represents a particular sound, with the result that when the endings change, the spelling of the stem must be altered to preserve the same sounds.

1) Verbs with a stem ending in *c, g* or *z* are regular in conjugation, but when the root begins with *e* or *i,* the spelling changes slightly.

(a) buscar   *to look for*
      sacar   *to take out*

INDICATIVO

Pretérito   busqué, buscaste, buscó, buscamos, buscasteis, buscaron
                     saqué, sacaste, sacó, sacamos, sacasteis, sacaron

SUBJUNTIVO

Presente   busque, busques, busque, busquemos, busquéis, busquen
                     saque, saques, saque, saquemos, saquéis, saquen

(b) ligar   *to tie*

INDICATIVO

Pretérito   ligué, ligaste, ligó, ligamos, ligasteis, ligaron

SUBJUNTIVO

Presente   ligue, ligues, ligue, liguemos, liguéis, liguen
            jugar and pagar follow the same pattern

(c) **llegar**   *to arrive*
     distinguir   *to distinguish*

INDICATIVO

Presente   llego, llegas, llega, llegamos, llegáis, llegan
                   distingo, distingues, distingue, distinguimos, distinguís,
                   distinguen
Pretérito   **llegué**, llegaste, llegó, llegamos, llegasteis, llegaron
                   distinguí, distinguiste, distinguió, distinguimos, distinguisteis,
                   distinguieron

SUBJUNTIVO

Presente   **llegue, llegues, llegue, lleguemos, lleguéis, lleguen**
                   **distinga, distingas, distinga, distingamos, distingáis,
                   distingan**

(d) **coger**   *to seize*

INDICATIVO

Presente   cojo, coges, coge, cogemos, cogéis, cogen

SUBJUNTIVO

Presente   coja, cojas, coja, cojamos, cojáis, cojan

Common verbs with the same pattern:

corregir	*to correct*	**fingir**	*to pretend*
dirigir	*to direct*	**proteger**	*to protect*
eligir	*to elect, choose*		

(e) **cazar**   *to hunt*

INDICATIVO

Presente   cazo, cazas, caza, cazamos, cazáis, cazan
Pretérito   **cacé**, cazaste, cazó, cazamos, cazasteis, cazaron

SUBJUNTIVO

Presente   cace, caces, cace, cacemos, cacéis, cacen

Common verbs with the same changes:

avergonzarse	*to be ashamed*	torcer	*twist*
cruzar	*to cross*	vencer	*to overcome*
forzar	*to force*		

2) Verbs ending in -ecer, -ocer, -acer and -ucir are irregular in the First Person Singular of the Present Indicative, and in all the Present Subjunctive:

conocer   *to know*

INDICATIVO

Presente   conozco, conoces, conoce, conocemos, conocéis, conocen

SUBJUNTIVO

Presente   conozca, conozcas, conozca, conozcamos, conozcáis,
                  conozcan

Common verbs with the same pattern:

agradecer	*to be grateful*	favorecer	*to favour*
aparecer	*to appear*	lucir	*to shine*
complacer	*to please*	merecer	*to merit*
compadecer	*to sympathise*	nacer	*to be born*
crecer	*to grow*	obedecer	*to obey*
desaparecer	*to disappear*	ofrecer	*to offer*
empobrecer	*to become poor*	padecer	*to suffer*
engrandecer	*to magnify*	parecer	*to seem*
enriquecer	*to become rich*	permanecer	*to remain*
envejecer	*to become old*	pertenecer	*to belong to*
establecer	*to establish*	reconocer	*to recognise*
fortalecer	*to strengthen*	yacer	*to lie*

For further notes on **yacer** see p. 47. For **mecer, cocer, esparcir** see p. 76, and for **satisfacer** p. 79.

3) Verbs ending in **-ducir** are similar to 2) above, but are also irregular in the Preterite and the Past Subjunctive:

traducir *to translate*

INDICATIVO

Presente   **traduzco, traduces, traduce, traducimos, traducís, traducen**

Pretérito   **traduje, tradujiste, tradujo, tradujimos, tradujisteis, tradujeron**

SUBJUNTIVO

Presente   **traduzca, traduzcas, traduzca, traduzcamos, traduzcáis, traduzcan**

Imperfecto   **tradujera, tradujeras, tradujera, tradujéramos, tradujerais, tradujeran**
tradujese, tradujeses, tradujese, tradujésemos, tradujeseis, tradujesen

Common verbs with the same pattern:

conducir	*to drive*	**producir**	*to produce*
deducir	*to deduce*	**reducir**	*to reduce*
introducir	*to introduce*	**seducir**	*to seduce*

4) Verbs ending in **-eer** have three irregular forms:

leer *to read*

Gerundio   **leyendo**

INDICATIVO

Pretérito   leí, leíste, **leyó,** leímos, leisteis, leyeron

SUBJUNTIVO

Imperfecto   **leyera, leyeras, leyera, leyéramos, leyérais, leyeran**
leyese, leyeses, leyese, leyésemos, leyeseis, leyesen

Common verbs with the same pattern:

creer	*to believe*	**proveer**	*to provide*
poseer	*to possess*	**roer**	*to gnaw*

Caer, oír and **traer** are similar (see pp. 63, 67, 72).

2) Verbs ending in **-uir** have the same irregularities, and in addition *i* becomes *y* between two vowels:

huir *to run away*

Gerundio **huyendo**

INDICATIVO

Presente **huyo, huyes, huye,** huimos, huís, **huyen**
Pretérito huí, huiste, **huyó,** huimos, huisteis, **huyeron**

SUBJUNTIVO

Presente **huya, huyas, huya, huyamos, huyáis, huyan**
Imperfecto **huyera, huyeras, huyera, huyéramos, huyerais, huyeran**
huyese, huyeses, huyese, huyésemos, huyeseis, huyesen

IMPERATIVO

tú **huye**

Common verbs with the same pattern:

argüir	*to argue*	**disminuir**	*to diminish*
atribuir	*to attribute*	**distribuir**	*to distribute*
concluir	*to conclude*	**excluir**	*to exclude*
constituir	*to constitute*	**incluir**	*to include*
construir	*to construct*	**influir**	*to influence*
contribuir	*to contribute*	**instituir**	*to institute*
destruir	*to destroy*	**restituir**	*to restore*
destituir	*to dismiss*	**sustituir**	*to substitute*

B. CHANGES IN STRESS

1) The accent in Spanish indicates when the stress in the pronunciation of word differs from the usual rules. This appears quite clearly in various parts of verbs ending in -iar and -uar.

(a) **cambiar**   *to change*

INDICATIVO

Presente   cambio, cambias, cambia, cambiamos, cambiáis, cambian

SUBJUNTIVO

Presente   cambie, cambies, cambie, cambiemos, cambiéis, cambien

Common verbs with the same pattern:

ajusticiar	*to execute*	financiar	*to finance*
aliviar	*to alleviate*	iniciar	*to begin*
apreciar	*to appreciate*	negociar	*to negotiate*
auspiciar	*to sponsor*	obsequiar	*to present*
beneficiar	*to benefit*	odiar	*to hate*
codiciar	*to covet*	pronunciar	*to pronounce*
desperdiciar	*to waste*	propiciar	*to favour*
depreciar	*to depreciate*	reconciliar	*to reconcile*
despreciar	*to look down on*	remediar	*to solve*
divorciar	*to divorce*	saciar	*to overdo*
estudiar	*to study*	silenciar	*to silence*
fastidiar	*to annoy*		

(b) **enviar**   *to send*

INDICATIVO

Presente   envío, envías, envía, enviamos, enviáis, envían

SUBJUNTIVO

Presente   envíe, envíes, envíe, enviemos, enviéis, envíen

59

Common verbs with the same pattern:

amnistiar	to amnesty	extraviar	to mislay
ampliar	to enlarge	fiar	to trust
criar	to breed	fotografiar	to photograph
confiar	to confide	guiar	to guide
contrariar	to contradict	mecanografiar	to type
desafiar	to distrust	taquigrafiar	to write shorthand
enfriar	to get cold	vaciar	to empty
espiar	to spy	variar	to vary
esquiar	to ski		

Useful guide:

without stressed *i*

aliviar	el alivio	*relief*
apreciar	el aprecio	*appreciation*
desperdiciar	el desperdicio	*waste*
estudiar	el estudio	*study*
iniciar	el inicio	*beginning*
odiar	el odio	*hatred*
remediar	el remedio	*remedy*
silenciar	el silencio	*silence*

with stressed *i*

desafiar	el desafío	*challenge*
enviar	el envío	*dispatch*
espiar	el espía	*spy*
fotografiar	la fotografía	*photograph*
enfriar	el frío	*cold*
guiar	el guía	*guide*
mecanografiar	la mecanografía	*typing*
vaciar	el vacío	*void*

(c) evacuar   *to evacuate*

INDICATIVO

Presente   evacuo, evacuas, evacua, evacuamos, evacuáis, evacuan

SUBJUNTIVO

Presente   evacue, evacues, evacue, evacuemos, evacuéis, evacuen

60

Common verbs with the same pattern:

amortiguar	*to deaden*	averiguar	*to verify*
apaciguar	*to soften*	atestiguar	*to testify*

Note: for more on **averiguar**, see p. 75.

(d) efectuar   *to carry out*

INDICATIVO

Presente   efectúo, efectúas, efectúa, efectuamos, efectuáis, efectúan

SUBJUNTIVO

Presente   efectúe, efectúes, efectúe, efectuemos, efectuéis, efectúen

Common verbs with the same pattern:

amenguar	*to diminish, wane*	evaluar	*to evaluate*
acentuar	*to accentuate*	exceptuar	*to except*
actuar	*to act*	fluctuar	*to fluctuate*
atenuar	*to attenuate*	perpetuar	*to perpetuate*
continuar	*to continue*	situar	*to locate*

2) Some verbs have an accent to prevent two vowels forming into a diphthong, and to make sure that both are pronounced quite separately:

(a) aislar   *to isolate*
     prohibir   *to prohibit*
     reunir   *to meet*

INDICATIVO

Presente   aíslo, aíslas, aísla, aislamos, aisláis, aíslan
                  prohíbo, prohíbes, prohíbe, prohibimos, prohibís,
                  prohíben
                  reúno, reúnes, reúne, reunimos, reunís, reúnen

SUBJUNTIVO

Presente   aísle, aísles, aísle, aislemos, aisléis, aíslen
                  prohíba, prohíbas, prohíba, prohibamos, prohibáis,
                  prohíban
                  reúna, reúnas, reúna, reunamos, reunáis, reúnan

61

10 Major Irregular Verbs

Andar

to walk

Infinitivo	andar
Gerundio	andando
Participio pasado	andado

INDICATIVO

Presente	ando, andas, anda, andamos, andáis, andan
Pretérito	**anduve, anduviste, anduvo, anduvimos, anduvisteis, anduvieron**
Imperfecto	andaba, andabas, andaba, andábamos, andabais, andaban
Futuro	andaré, andarás, andará, andaremos, andaréis, andarán
Condicional	andaría, andarías, andaría, andaríamos, andaríais, andarían

SUBJUNTIVO

Presente	ande, andes, ande, andemos, andéis, anden
Imperfecto	**anduviera, anduvieras, anduviera, anduviéramos, anduvierais, anduvieran, anduviese, anduvieses, anduviese, anduviésemos, anduvieseis, anduviesen**

IMPERATIVO

tú	anda
vosotros	andad

Caber

to fit

Infinitivo	caber
Gerundio	cabiendo
Participio pasado	cabido

INDICATIVO

Presente	**quepo,** cabes, cabe, cabemos, cabéis, caben
Pretérito	**cupe, cupiste, cupo, cupimos, cupisteis, cupieron**

Imperfecto	cabía, cabías, cabía, cabíamos, cabíais, cabían
Futuro	cabré, cabrás, cabrá, cabremos, cabréis, cabrán
Condicional	cabría, cabrías, cabría, cabríamos, cabríais, cabrían

SUBJUNTIVO

Presente	quepa, quepas, quepa, quepamos, quepáis, quepan
Imperfecto	cupiera, cupieras, cupiera, cupiéramos, cupiérais, cupieran
	cupiese, cupieses, cupiese, cupiésemos, cupieseis, cupiesen

IMPERATIVO

| tú | cabe |
| vosotros | cabed |

caer   *to fall*

Infinitivo	caer
Gerundio	cayendo
Participio pasado	caído

INDICATIVO

Presente	caigo, caes, cae, caemos, caéis, caen
Pretérito	caí, caíste, cayó, caímos, caísteis, cayeron
Imperfecto	caía, caías, caía, caíamos, caíais, caían
Futuro	caeré, caerás, caerá, caeremos, caeréis, caerán
Condicional	caería, caerías, caería, caeríamos, caeríais, caerían

SUBJUNTIVO

Presente	caiga, caigas, caiga, caigamos, caigáis, caigan
Imperfecto	cayera, cayeras, cayera, cayéramos, cayerais, cayeran
	cayese, cayeses, cayese, cayésemos, cayeseis, cayesen

IMPERATIVO

| tú | cae |
| vosotros | caed |

Dar   *to give*

Infinitivo	dar
Gerundio	dando
Participio pasado	dado

INDICATIVO

Presente	**doy, das, da, damos, dais, dan**
Pretérito	**di, diste, dio, dimos, disteis, dieron**
Imperfecto	daba, dabas, daba, dábamos, dabais, daban
Futuro	daré, darás, dará, daremos, daréis, darán
Condicional	daría, darías, daría, daríamos, daríais, darían

SUBJUNTIVO

Presente	**dé, des, dé, demos, deis, den**
Imperfecto	**diera, dieras, diera, diéramos, dierais, dieran**
	diese, dieses, diese, diésemos, dieseis, diesen

IMPERATIVO

tú	**da**
vosotros	**dad**

You may sometimes see an accent on monosyllabic forms, like di, dio, fui, fue and vi, vio; but the Real Academia Española decided in 1952 that no accent was necessary. Dé has an accent simply to prevent confusion with de, meaning *of*.

Decir

to say, tell

Infinitivo	**decir**
Gerundio	**diciendo**
Participio pasado	**dicho**

INDICATIVO

Presente	**digo, dices, dice,** decimos, decís, **dicen**
Pretérito	**dije, dijiste, dijo, dijimos, dijisteis, dijeron**
Imperfecto	decía, decías, decía, decíamos, decíais, decían
Futuro	**diré, dirás, dirá, diremos, diréis, dirán**
Condicional	**diría, dirías, diría, diríamos, diríais, dirían**

SUBJUNTIVO

Presente	**diga, digas, diga, digamos, digáis, digan**
Imperfecto	**dijera, dijeras, dijera, dijéramos, dijerais, dijeran**
	dijese, dijeses, dijese, dijésemos, dijeseis, dijesen

| tú | di |
| vosotros | decid |

See p. 76 for details of irregular compound forms of *decir*.

Estar   *to be*

Infinitivo	estar
Gerundio	estando
Participio pasado	estado

INDICATIVO

Presente	**estoy, estás, está, estamos, estáis, están**
Pretérito	**estuve, estuviste, estuvo, estuvimos, estuvisteis, estuvieron**
Imperfecto	estaba, estabas, estaba, estábamos, estabais, estaban
Futuro	estaré, estarás, estará, estaremos, estaréis, estarán
Condicional	estaría, estarías, estaría, estaríamos, estaríais, estarían

SUBJUNTIVO

Presente	esté, estés, esté, estemos, estéis, estén
Imperfecto	**estuviera, estuvieras, estuviera, estuviéramos, estuvierais, estuvieran**
	estuviese, estuvieses, estuviese, estuviésemos, estuvieseis, estuviesen

IMPERATIVO

| tú | está |
| vosotros | estad |

Haber   *to have* (Auxiliary)

Infinitivo	haber
Gerundio	habiendo
Participio pasado	habido

INDICATIVO

| Presente | **he, has, ha, hemos,** habéis, **han** |

Pretérito	hube, hubiste, hubo, hubimos, hubisteis, hubieron
Imperfecto	había, habías, había, habíamos, habíais, habían
Futuro	habré, habrás, habrá, habremos, habréis, habrán
Condicional	habría, habrías, habría, habríamos, habríais, habrían

SUBJUNTIVO

Presente	haya, hayas, haya, hayamos, hayáis, hayan
Imperfecto	hubiera, hubieras, hubiera, hubiéramos, hubierais, hubieran
	hubiese, hubieses, hubiese, hubiésemos, hubieseis, hubiesen

IMPERATIVO

| tú | he |
| vosotros | habed |

Note: **he aquí** = *here is*

Hacer

to do, make

Infinitivo	hacer
Gerundio	haciendo
Participio pasado	hecho

INDICATIVO

Presente	hago, haces, hace, hacemos, hacéis, hacen
Pretérito	hice, hiciste, hizo, hicimos, hicisteis, hicieron
Imperfecto	hacía, hacías, hacía, hacíamos, hacíais, hacían
Futuro	haré, harás, hará, haremos, haréis, harán
Condicional	haría, harías, haría, haríamos, haríais, harían

SUBJUNTIVO

Presente	haga, hagas, haga, hagamos, hagáis, hagan
Imperfecto	hiciera, hicieras, hiciera, hiciéramos, hicierais, hicieran
	hiciese, hicieses, hiciese, hiciésemos, hicieseis, hiciesen

IMPERATIVO

| tú | haz |
| vosotros | haced |

Note: see p. 79 for details of irregular compound forms of **hacer**.

66

Ir

Infinitivo	ir
Gerundio	**yendo**
Participio pasado	ido

INDICATIVO

Presente	**voy, vas, va, vamos, vais, van**
Pretérito	**fui, fuiste, fue, fuimos, fuisteis, fueron**
Imperfecto	**iba, ibas, iba, íbamos, ibais, iban**
Futuro	iré, irás, irá, iremos, iréis, irán
Condicional	iría, irías, iría, iríamos, iríais, irían

SUBJUNTIVO

Presente	**vaya, vayas, vaya, vayamos, vayáis, vayan**
Imperfecto	**fuera, fueras, fuera, fuéramos, fuerais, fueran**
	fuese, fueses, fuese, fuésemos, fueseis, fuesen

IMPERATIVO

tú	**ve**
vosotros	id

Note: **ir** and **ser** have identical forms in the Preterite, and the Imperfect Subjunctive.

Oír

to hear

Infinitivo	oír
Gerundio	**oyendo**
Participio pasado	oído

INDICATIVO

Presente	**oigo, oyes, oye,** oímos, oís, **oyen**
Pretérito	oí, oíste, **oyó,** oímos, oisteis, **oyeron**
Imperfecto	oía, oías, oía, oíamos, oíais, oían
Futuro	oiré, oirás, oirá, oiremos, oiréis, oirán
Condicional	oiría, oirías, oiría, oiríamos, oiríais, oirían

SUBJUNTIVO

Presente	**oiga, oigas, oiga, oigamos, oigáis, oigan**

| Imperfecto | oyera, oyeras, oyera, oyéramos, oyerais, oyeran |
| | oyese, oyeses, oyese, oyésemos, oyeseis, oyesen |

IMPERFECTO

| tú | oye |
| vosotros | oíd |

Poder   *to be able*

Infinitivo	poder
Gerundio	pudiendo
Participio pasado	podido

INDICATIVO

Presente	puedo, puedes, puede, podemos, podéis, pueden
Pretérito	pude, pudiste, pudo, pudimos, pudisteis, pudieron
Imperfecto	podía, podías, podía, podíamos, podíais, podían
Futuro	podré, podrás, podrá, podremos, podréis, podrán
Condicional	podría, podrías, podría, podríamos, podríais, podrían

SUBJUNTIVO

Presente	pueda, puedas, pueda, podamos, podáis, puedan
Imperfecto	pudiera, pudieras, pudiera, pudiéramos, pudierais,
	pudieran
	pudiese, pudieses, pudiese, pudiésemos, pudieseis,
	pudiesen

Poner   *to put*

Indicativo	poner
Gerundio	poniendo
Participio pasado	**puesto**

INDICATIVO

Presente	pongo, pones, pone, ponemos, ponéis, ponen
Pretérito	puse, pusiste, puso, pusimos, pusisteis, pusieron
Imperfecto	ponía, ponías, ponía, poníamos, poníais, ponían
Futuro	pondré, pondrás, pondrá, pondremos, pondréis, pondrán
Condicional	pondría, pondrías, pondría, pondríamos, pondríais,
	pondrían

Presente	ponga, pongas, ponga, pongamos, pongáis, pongan
Imperfecto	pusiera, pusieras, pusiera, pusiéramos, pusierais, pusieran
	pusiese, pusieses, pusiese, pusiésemos, pusieseis, pusiesen

IMPERATIVO

tú	pon
vosotros	poned

Querer   *to want, love*

Infinitivo	querer
Gerundio	queriendo
Participio pasado	querido

INDICATIVO

Presente	quiero, quieres, quiere, queremos, queréis, quieren
Pretérito	quise, quisiste, quiso, quisimos, quisisteis, quisieron
Imperfecto	quería, querías, quería, queríamos, queríais, querían
Futuro	querré, querrás, querrá, querremos, querréis, querrán
Condicional	querría, querrías, querría, querríamos, querríais, querrían

SUBJUNTIVO

Presente	quiera, quieras, quiera, quieramos, quieráis, quieran
Imperfecto	quisiera, quisieras, quisiera, quisiéramos, quisierais, quisieran
	quisiese, quisieses, quisiese, quisiésemos, quisieseis, quisiesen

Note: Despite the resemblance of certain forms of **adquirir, inquirir** (*to acquire, to inquire*) to **querer** (adquiero, inquiero, etc.) they are not in fact compounds and do not have the same irregular forms (e.g. **adquirido, inquirí**).

Saber   *to know*

Infinitivo	saber
Gerundio	sabiendo
Participio pasado	sabido

INDICATIVO

Presente	sé, sabes, sabe, sabemos, sabéis, saben

Pretérito	supe, supiste, supo, supimos, supisteis, supieron
Imperfecto	sabía, sabías, sabía, sabíamos, sabíais, sabían
Futuro	sabré, sabrás, sabrá, sabremos, sabréis, sabrán
Condicional	sabría, sabrías, sabría, sabríamos, sabríais, sabrían

SUBJUNTIVO

Presente	sepa, sepas, sepa, sepamos, sepáis, sepan
Imperfecto	supiera, supieras, supiera, supiéramos, supieriais, supieran
	supiese, supieses, supiese, supiésemos, supieseis, supiesen

IMPERATIVO

tú	sabe
vosotros	sabed

Salir

to leave

Infinitivo	salir
Gerundio	saliendo
Participio pasado	salido

INDICATIVO

Presente	salgo, sales, sale, salimos, salís, salen
Pretérito	salí, saliste, salió, salimos, salisteis, salieron
Imperfecto	salía, salías, salía, salíamos, salíais, salían
Futuro	saldré, saldrás, saldrá, saldremos, saldréis, saldrán
Condicional	saldría, saldrías, saldría, saldríamos, saldríais, saldrían

SUBJUNTIVO

Presente	salga, salgas, salga, salgamos, salgáis, salgan
Imperfecto	saliera, salieras, saliera, saliéramos, salierais, salieran
	saliese, salieses, saliese, saliésemos, salieseis, saliesen

IMPERATIVO

tú	sal
vosotros	salid

Ser

to be

Infinitivo	ser
Gerundio	siendo
Participio pasado	sido

INDICATIVO

Presente	soy, eres, es, somos, sois, son
Pretérito	fui, fuiste, fue, fuimos, fuisteis, fueron
Imperfecto	era, eras, era, éramos, érais, eran
Futuro	seré, serás, será, seremos, seréis, serán
Condicional	sería, serías, sería, seríamos, seríais, serían

SUBJUNTIVO

Presente	sea, seas, sea, seamos, seáis, sean
Imperfecto	fuera, fueras, fuera, fuéramos, fuerais, fueran
	fuese, fueses, fuese, fuésemos, fueseis, fuesen

IMPERATIVO

tú	sé
vosotros	sed

Tener

to have

Inifinitivo	tener
Gerundio	teniendo
Participio pasado	tenido

INDICATIVO

Presente	tengo, tienes, tiene, tenemos, tenéis, tienen
Pretérito	tuve, tuviste, tuvo, tuvimos, tuvisteis, tuvieron
Imperfecto	tenía, tenías, tenía, teníamos, teníais, tenían
Futuro	tendré, tendrás, tendrá, tendremos, tendréis, tendrán
Condicional	tendría, tendrías, tendría, tendríamos, tendríais, tendrían

SUBJUNTIVO

Presente	tenga, tengas, tenga, tengamos, tengáis, tengan
Imperfecto	tuviera, tuvieras, tuviera, tuviéramos, tuvierais, tuvieran
	tuviese, tuvieses, tuviese, tuviésemos, tuvieseis, tuviesen

71

IMPERATIVO

| tú | ten |
| vosotros | tened |

Traer   *to bring*

Infinitivo	traer
Gerundio	**trayendo**
Participio pasado	traído

INDICATIVO

Presente	**traigo, traes, trae, traemos, traéis, traen**
Pretérito	**traje, trajiste, trajo, trajimos, trajisteis, trajeron**
Imperfecto	traía, traías, traía, traíamos, traíais, traían
Futuro	traeré, traerás, traerá, traeremos, traeréis, traerán
Condicional	traería, traerías, traería, traeríamos, traeríais, traerían

SUBJUNTIVO

Presente	**traiga, traigas, traiga, traigamos, traigáis, traigan**
Imperfecto	**trajera, trajeras, trajera, trajéramos, trajerais, trajeran**
	trajese, trajeses, trajese, trajésemos, trajeseis, trajesen

IMPERATIVO

| tú | trae |
| vosotros | traed |

Venir   *to come*

Infinitivo	venir
Gerundio	viniendo
Participio pasado	venido

INDICATIVO

Presente	**vengo, vienes, viene, venimos, venís, vienen**
Pretérito	**vine, viniste, vino, vinimos, vinisteis, vinieron**
Imperfecto	venía, venías, venía, veníamos, veníais, venían
Futuro	**vendré, vendrás, vendrá, vendremos, vendréis, vendrán**
Condicional	**vendría, vendrías, vendría, vendríamos, vendríais, vendrían**

Presente	venga, vengas, venga, vengamos, vengáis, vengan
Imperfecto	viniera, vinieras, viniera, viniéramos, vinierais, vinieran
	viniese, vinieses, viniese, viniésemos, vinieseis, viniesen

IMPERATIVO

tú	ven
vosotros	venid

Ver   *to see*

Infinitivo	ver
Gerundio	viendo
Participio pasado	visto

INDICATIVO

Presente	veo, ves, ve, vemos, véis, ven
Pretérito	vi, viste, vio, vimos, visteis, vieron
Imperfecto	veía, veías, veía, veíamos, veíais, veían
Futuro	veré, verás, verá, veremos, veréis, verán
Condicional	vería, verías, vería, veríamos, veríais, verían

SUBJUNTIVO

Presente	vea, veas, vea, veamos, veáis, vean
Imperfecto	viera, vieras, viera, viéramos, vierais, vieran
	viese, vieses, viese, viésemos, vieseis, viesen

IMPERATIVO

tú	ve
vosotros	ved

11 Minor Irregularities

A. PAST PARTICIPLES

1) Irregular Forms

abrir	*to open*	abierto	imprimir	*to print*	impreso
cubrir	*to cover*	cubierto	morir	*to die*	muerto
decir	*to say*	dicho	poner	*to put*	puesto
disolver	*to dissolve*	disuelto	resolver	*to resolve*	resuelto
escribir	*to write*	escrito	romper	*to break*	roto
hacer	*to do, make*	hecho	ver	*to see*	visto
			volver	*to return*	vuelto

2) Verbs with both Regular and Irregular Past Participles

		Regular	*Irregular*
abstraer	*to abstract*	abstraído	abstracto
bendecir	*to bless*	bendecido	bendito
freír	*to fry*	freído	frito
prender	*to take*	prendido	preso
proveer	*to provide*	proveído	provisto

3) Verbs with a Regular Past Participle and a Related Adjective

		Participle	*Adjective*	
corregir	*to correct*	corregido	correcto	*correct*
defender	*to defend*	defendido	indefenso	*defenceless*
desertar	*to desert*	desertado	desierto	*abandoned*
despertar	*to wake*	despertado	despierto	*awake*
distinguir	*to distinguish*	distinguido	distinto	*different*
divergir	*to diverge*	divergido	diverso	*divers*
exceptuar	*to make an exception*	exceptuado	excepto	*except*
eximir	*to exempt*	eximido	exento	*exempt*

74

		Participle	*Adjective*	
expresar	*to express*	expresado	expreso	*express*
extender	*to extend*	extendido	extenso	*extensive*
disolver	*to dissolve*	disuelto	disoluto	*dissolute*
favorecer	*to favour*	favorecido	favorito	*favourite*
fijar	*to fix*	fijado	fijo	*fixed*
incluir	*to include*	incluido	incluso	*even*
juntar	*to join, add*	junto (-ado)	adjunto	*enclosed*
maldecir	*to curse*	maldecido	maldito	*damned*
medir	*to measure*	medido	inmenso	*immense*
molestar	*to annoy, disturb*	molestado	molesto	*annoyed*
nacer	*to be born*	nacido	nato	*inherent*
presumir	*to boast*	presumido	presunto	*presumed*
resolver	*to resolve*	resuelto	resoluto	*resolute*
situarse	*to be placed*	situado	sito	*sited*
soltar	*to release*	soltado	suelto	*loose*
tender	*to stretch*	tendido	tenso	*tense*
teñir	*to dye*	teñido	tinto	*tinged, red (wine)*

B. MISCELLANEOUS FORMS

1) Asir
to grasp

Presente de Indicativo asgo, ases, ase, asimos, asís, asen

Presente de Subjuntivo asga, asgas, asga, asgamos, asgáis, asgan

2) Avergonzarse
to be ashamed

Presente de Indicativo me avergüenzo, te avergüenzas, se avergüenza, nos avergonzamos, os avergonzáis, se avergüenzan

Presente de Subjuntivo me avergüence, te avergüences, se avergüence, nos avergoncemos, os avergoncéis, se avergüencen

3) Averiguar
to verify

In order to preserve the correct pronunciation, the diaeresis (¨) is used in the Preterite and Present Subjunctive:

Pretérito averigüé, averiguaste, averiguó, averiguamos, averiguasteis, averiguaron

Presente de Subjuntivo averigüe, averigües, averigüe, averigüemos, averigüéis, averigüen

4) Cocer   *to cook*
   Mecer   *to rock*

Although they end in -ocer *and* -ecer these verbs do not follow the pattern on p. 56:

Presente de Indicativo	cuezo, cueces, cuece, cocemos, cocéis, cuecen
	mezo, meces, mece, mecemos, mecéis, mecen
Presente de Subjuntivo	cueza, cuezas, cueza, cozamos, cozáis, cuezan
	meza, meza, meza, mezamos, mezáis, mezan
Imperativo	cuece, coced
	mece, meced

Note: **esparcir,** *to scatter,* follows the same pattern as **mecer.**

5) Bendecir   *to bless*
   Contradecir   *to contradict*
   Maldecir   *to curse*
   Predecir   *to foretell*

These compounds of **decir** have the same irregularities as the verb they derive from, with the following exceptions:

Imperativo	contradice	maldice
	bendice	predice
Futuro	bendeciré	maldeciré
	contradeciré	predeciré
Condicional	bendeciría	maldeciría
	contradeciría	prediciría
Participio pasado	bendecido	maldecido

6) **Erguir**   *to set up straight*

Alternative forms exist in certain tenses:

Presente de Indicativo	irgo, irgues, irgue, erguimos, erguís, irguen
	(NB: this is rather archaic)
OR	yergo, yergues, yergue, erguimos, erguís, yerguen
Presente de Subjuntivo	irga, irgas, irga, irgamos, irgáis, irgan
OR	yerga, yergas, yerga, yergamos, yergáis, yergan
Imperativo	irgue OR yergue, erguid
Imperfecto de Subjuntivo	irguiera, irguieras, irguiera, irguiéramos,
	irguierais, irguieran
	irguiese, irguieses, irguiese, irguiésemos,
	irguieseis, irguiesen

Note: these are the only forms for the Imperfect Subjunctive.

7) Errar   *to err*

The letter **y** also intrudes in certain tenses here, but without alternatives:

Presente de Indicativo	**yerro, yerras, yerra,** erramos, erráis, **yerran**
Present de Subjuntivo	**yerre, yerres, yerre,** erremos, erréis, **yerren**
Imperativo	**yerra,** errad

8) Oler   *to smell*

Oler follows the same changes as **mover** (see p. 52), with these exceptions:

Presente de Indicative	**huelo, hueles, huele,** olemos, oléis, **huelen**
Presente de Subjuntivo	**huela, huelas, huela,** olamos, oláis, **huelan**
Imperativo	**huele,** oled

9) Prever   *to foresee*

This is a compound of **ver** (see p. 73), but there is a change in stress, marked by accents:

Presente de Indicativo	**preveo, prevés, prevé,** prevemos, prevéis, **prevén**

10) Pudrir   *to decay*

Similar to verbs like **dormir** (see p. 53) but with these changes:

Presente de Indicativo	pudro, pudres, pudre, pudrimos **OR podrimos,** pudrís **OR podrís,** pudren
Pretérito	**podrí,** podriste, pudrió, **podrimos, podristeis,** pudrieron
Presente de Subjuntivo	**pudra, pudras, pudra,** pudramos, pudráis, **pudran**

10) Reír   *to laugh*
Sonreír   *to smile*

Conjugated like **pedir** (see p. 50), but the **i** of any ending is dropped when the stem also ends in **i**:

Gerundio	**riendo**
	sonriendo

77

Presente de Indicativo	río, ríes, ríe, reímos, reís, ríen
	sonrío, sonríes, sonríe, sonreímos, sonreís,
	sonríen
Pretérito	reí, reíste, rió, reímos, reísteis, rieron
	sonreí, sonreíste, sonrió, sonreímos, sonreisteis,
	sonrieron
Presente de Subjuntivo	ría, rías, ría, ríamos, riáis, rían
	sonría, sonrías, sonría, sonríamos, sonriáis,
	sonrían
Imperfecto de Subjuntivo	riera, rieras, riera, riéramos, rierais, rieran
	sonriera, sonrieras, sonriera, sonriéramos,
	sonrierais, sonrieran
	riese, rieses, riese, riésemos, rieseis, riesen
	sonriese, sonrieses, sonriese, sonriésemos,
	sonrieseis, sonriesen
Imperativo	ríe, reíd
	sonríe, sonreíd

12) **Reñir**   *to quarrel*
     Bullir   *to boil*

Follows **pedir** (see p. 50), but these verbs with a stem ending in ñ, and those ending in ll, drop the i in any endings where the i is without an accent:

Gerundio	riñendo
	bullendo
Presente de Indicativo	riño, riñes, riñe, reñimos, reñís, riñen
	bullo, bulles, bulle, bullimos, bullís, bullen
Pretérito	reñí, reñiste, riñó, reñimos, reñisteis, riñeron
	bullí, bulliste, bulló, bullimos, bullisteis, bulleron
Presente de Subjuntivo	riña, riñas, riña, riñamos, riñáis, riñan
Imperfecto de Subjuntivo	riñese, riñeses, riñese, riñésemos, riñeseis, riñesen
	bullese, bulleses, bullese, bullésemos, bulleseis,
	bullesen
	riñera, riñeras, riñera, riñéramos, riñerais, riñeran
	bullera, bulleras, bullera, bulléramos, bullérais,
	bulleran
Imperativo	riñe, reñid
	bulle, bullid

Other verbs in this group:

bruñir	*to burnish*	henchir	*to swell up*
ceñir	*to surround*	teñir	*to dye*
constreñir	*to restrict*	tullir	*to paralyse*
gruñir	*to growl*	zambullir	*to dip*

13) Satisfacer   *to satisfy*

Similar to **hacer** (see p. 66), **satisfacer** has the following differences:

Gerundio	satisfaciendo
Participio pasado	satisfecho
Presente de Indicativo	satisfago, satisfaces, satisface, satisfacemos, satisfacéis, satisfacen
Imperfecto	satisfacía, satisfacías, satisfacía, satisfacíamos, satisfacíais, satisfacían
Pretérito	satisfice, satisficiste, satisfizo, satisficimos, satisficisteis, satisficieron
Futuro	satisfaré, satisfarás, satisfará, satisfaremos, satisfaréis, satisfarán
Condicional	satisfaría, satisfarías, satisfaría, satisfaríamos, satisfaríais, satisfarían
Presente de Subjuntivo	satisfaga, satisfagas, satisfaga, satisfagamos, satisfagáis, satisfagan
Imperfecto de Subjuntivo	satisficiera, satisficieras, satisficiera, satisficiéramos, satisficierais, satisficieran satisficiese, satisficieses, satisficiese, satisficiésemos, satisficieseis, satisficiesen
Imperativo	satisfaz, satisfaced

Index of Vocabulary

actual, present
afectar, to have an impact on
ahora, now
al respecto, on that subject
allí, there
antes de, before
apenas, scarcely, hardly
aun no, not yet
avión, *m,* aircraft
bastante, enough, quite a lot of
CEE, Comunidad Económica Europea,
   EEC
café, *m,* cafe
camino, way, road
catalán, *m and adj,* inhabitant of Catalonia,
   NE Spain
causar, to cause
Colón, Christopher Columbus
compañía, *m,* company;—Catalana,
   Catalan army in Greece, 14th Century
conducta, *f,* conduct, behaviour
Conquistadores, *m,* the Conquistadors
   (*historical*)
contestar, to answer
copa, *f,* glass
Correos, *m,* Post Office
correr, to run
Cortes Generales, *f,* Spanish
   Parliament
coyuntura, *f,* situation
crisis, *f,* crisis
cuestión, *f,* question, matter
Dalí, Salvador, Spanish painter
de parte de, on the part of
deber, to have to
declaración, *f,* declaration
desayuno, *m,* breakfast
después, after
Dios, *m,* God
dirigir, to direct
discordia, *f,* disagreement
económico, *adj,* economic
elecciones, *f,* elections
en cuanto a, with regard to
en seguida, straightaway
error, *m,* error
escribir, to write, a máquina, to
   typewrite

España, *f,* Spain
esperar, to wait, hope, expect
estación, *f,* station
estar, to be
   — de embajador, to be acting as
     ambassador
   — de guardia, to be on guard
   — de luto, to be in mourning
   — de prisa, to be in a
     hurry
   — de vacaciones, to be on holiday
   — de viaje, to be travelling
este, this
estilo, *m,* style
estimado, *adj,* dear (*letterwriting*)
esto, this
estos, estas, these
estudiar, to study
examinar, to examine
éxito, *m,* success
experto, *m,* expert
explicar, to explain
exportar, to export
exposición, *f,* exhibition
expulsar, to expel
familia, *f,* family
feria de muestras, *f,* samples trade
   fair
formulario de solicitud, *m,* application
   form
gente, *f,* people
gerente, *m,* manager
giro postal, *m,* postal order
gobierno, *m,* government
gracias, thank you
Gran Bretaña, *f,* Great Britain
gritar, to shout
guapo, *adj,* good-looking
haber, to have (*auxiliary*), — de, to
   have to, — que, to have to
hablar, to speak
hacer, to do, make
   — falta, to be necessary
haga el favor de, please be so kind
hallar, to find
hasta que, until
herido, *adj,* wounded
hermano, *m,* brother

hervir, to boil
hielo, *m*, ice
hora, *f*, hour, time
hotel, *m*, hotel
huelga, *f*, strike
idioma, *m*, language
imposible, *adj*, impossible
Inca, *m*, Inca (*civilisation in Peru*)
inestable, *adj*, unstable
informe, *m*, report, information
ingeniero jefe, *m*, chief engineer
ingrediente, *m*, ingredient
ingresar, to join
inhabilitarse, to become incapable (*legal*)
inscribirse, to enroll
instalación, *f*, installation
instante, *m*, moment
intervenir, to intervene
ir, to go
jefe, *m*, boss, — de publicidad, *m*, Head of
  Publicity, ingeniero —, *m*, Chief Engineer,
  —, *m*, de Ventas, *Head of Sales*
judío, *m*, jew
juguete, *m*, toy
junta, *f*, committee, military junta
justo, just
lavar, to wash
levantarse, to get up
librar, to free
libro, *m*, book
licuar, to liquidize
limón, *m*, lemon
lío, *m*, trouble
listo, *adj*, ready, intelligent
llamar, to call
— por teléfono, to give a ring
llegar, to arrive
llevar, to carry
luego, then, — que, after
luna, *f*, moon
maleta, *f*, suitcase
mañana, *f*, tomorrow; morning
mandar, to send, order
manzana, *f*, apple
matar, to kill
materia, *f*, subject, — prima, *f*, raw material
mayor de edad, *adj*, of age (*legal*)
médico, *m*, doctor
medidas, *f*, measures
menester, *m*, need, ser —, to need
mes, *m*, month
México, *m*, Mexico
mezclar, to mix
mientras, while
militar, *adj*, military
militar, *m*, soldier, officer
minuto, *m*, minute

mío, mine
mismo, *adj*, él —, himself, ella — a, herself
Moctezuma, Emperor of Mexico when the
  Spaniards arrived
motivo, *m*, motive
muchacha, *f*, girl
mucho, a lot of
muerto, *adj*, dead
Museo de Antropología, *m*, Anthropology
  Museum (*in Mexico City*)
musulmán, *m*, moslem
mutuo, *adj*, mutual
muy, very
negar, to deny
nevar, to snow
niño, *m*, child
no bien, as soon as
nombrar, to appoint
nombre, *m*, name
norteamericano, *m and adj*, U.S.
nosotros, -as, we
nuevo, *adj*, new
obra, *f*, work, building site
ocho, eight
ocupación, *f*, occupation
ocupado, *adj*, busy
oferta, *f*, offer
oficial *adj*, official
oficina, *f*, office
oír, to hear
ojalá, let's hope
opinión, *f*, opinion
padre, *m*, father
padres, *m*, parents
pagar por adelantado, to pay in advance
para, in order to, for
parecer, to seem
pared, *f*, wall
participar, to take part
partir, to leave
pasear, to go for a walk, salir a —,
  to go out for a walk
paz, *f*, peace
película, *f*, film
pensar, to think
perder el tren, to miss the train
perdón, excuse me
permiso, *m*, permit, — de
  importación, *m*, import licence
permitir, to allow, me permite, may I
perro, *m*, dog
peruano, Peruvian
pesar, to weigh, —, *m*, grief
pieza de repuesto, *f*, spare part
Pisco Sour, Peruvian cocktail
planta, *f*, plant
plástico, *m*, plastic

81

Plaza de España, square in Madrid
poder, *m,* power, — (*verb*), to be able
poderes públicos, *m,* Public
  Authorities
poderoso, powerful
poner, to quit
ponerse a, to begin to
por medio de, by means of
¿por qué?, why?; porque, because
posibilidad, *f,* possibility, chance
posible, possible
práctico, *adj,* practical
preciso, *adj,* essential
preferir, to prefer
preparativos de emergencia, *f,*
  emergency precautions
presente, *f,* this letter (*letterwriting*)
presidente, *m,* president
príncipe, *m,* prince
profesor, *m,* teacher
prohibir, to forbid, se prohíbe la
  entrada, no entry
prometer, to promise
promover, to promote, encourage
proponer, to propose
proyectar, to plan
proyecto, *m,* project
publicar, to publish
puesto, *m,* post, job
punto de vista, *m,* viewpoint
puntual, *adj,* punctual
quedar, to remain
quehaceres, *m,* jobs to do
quejarse de, to complain
querer, to want, love
queso, *m,* cheese
quienquiera, whoever
quizá(s), perhaps
razonable, *adj,* reasonable
recepcionista, *f,* receptionist
recíproco, *adj,* mutual, reciprocal
reconocer, to recognise
recordar, to remember
reemplazar, to replace
reloj, *m,* wristwatch
repetir, to repeat
reportaje, *m,* report
requerir, to require
respuesta, *f,* answer
resultado, *m,* result
retirarse, to retire
retrato, *m,* portrait
reunión, *f,* meeting
rey, *m,* king
romper, to break, burst
saber, to know
salir, to leave

secretaria, *f,* secretary
seguir, to follow, keep on
seis, six
sentarse, to sit down
ser, to be, — preciso, to be essential
servicio, *m,* service
servir, to serve
si, if; sí, yes, oneself
siempre, always
siete, seven
siglo, *m,* century
simpático, adj, **pleasant**
sin embargo, however
sin que, without
situación, *f,* situation
soldado, *m,* soldier
solicitar, to apply for
suponer, to suppose,
suspender, to suspend
tal, such
  — vez, perhaps
Talgo, *m,* famous express train
tardar, to be late
tarde, late
tarde, *f,* afternoon
tarea, *f,* task
teatro, *m,* theatre
telefonear, to telephone
teléfono, *m,* telephone
temer, to fear
tener, to have, — éxito, to be a success,
  — que, to have to
terminar, to finish
tía, aunt
tomar, to take, tomar en cuenta, to take into
  account
trabajar, to work
traje, *m,* suit
tren, *m,* train
tú, you, tu, your
tutelar, to supervise
uno, one, el — al otro, each other
urgente, *adj,* urgent
usted, you (*sing.*), ustedes, you (*plural*)
vender, to sell
venir, to come
ventana, *f,* window
ver, to see
vestirse, to get dressed
vino, *m,* wine
visitar, to visit
vivir, to live
vivo, adj, quick-witted, alive
volver, to return
vos, you (*sing.*)
vosotro, -as, you (*pl.*)
yo, I

Index of Regular Verb Endings

Index of Irregular Verbs

To identify an irregular part of any verb, look for the root in this Index. Remember that the ending may also be irregular! In which case, look in the Irregular Endings Index. Some verbs are monosyllabic (e.g. ver) and you will find those listed under a single letter. This index also includes those parts of verbs which have special accents.

crezc, > *crecer, p. 56*
crí/cri-, > *criar, p. 60*
cruc-, > *cruzar, p. 56*
cubiert-, > *cubrir, p. 74*
cuez-, > *cocer, p. 52, 76*
cuelg-, > *colgar, p. 52*
cuent-, > *contar, p. 52*
cuest-, > *costar, p. 52*
cuez-, > *cocer, p. 52, 76*
cup-, > *caber, p. 62*
deduj-, > *deducir, p. 57*
deduzc-, > *deducir, p. 57*
defiend-, > *defender, p. 48, 74*
demuestr-, > *demostrar, p. 52*
depreci-, > *depreciar, p. 59*
derrit-, > *derretir, p. 50*
desafí/desafi-, > *desafiar, p. 60*
desaparezc-, > *desaparecer, p. 56*
desaprueb-, > *desaprobar, p. 52*
desciend-, > *descender, p. 48*
desperdici-, > *desperdiciar, p. 59*
despid-, > *despedirse, p. 50*
despiert-, > *despertar, p. 48, 74*
despreci-, > *despreciar, p. 59*
destierr-, > *desterrar, p. 49*
destituy-, > *destituir, p. 58*
destruy-, > *destruir, p. 58*
devuelv-, > *devolver, p. 52*
di, > *dar, p. 64*
di, > *decir, p. 65*
dic-, > *decir, p. 64*
dicho-, > *decir, p. 64, 74*
die,- > *dar, p. 64*
difier-, > *diferir, p. 51*
dig-, > *decir, p. 64*
dij-, > *decir, p. 64*
dir-, > *decir, p. 64*
dirij-, > *dirigir, p. 55*
disminuy-, > *disminuir, p. 58*
disting-, > *distinguir, p. 55*
distingu-, > *distinguir, p. 55, 74*
distribuy-, > *distribuir, p. 58*
disuelt-, > *disolver, p. 74, 75*
diviert-, > *divertirse, p. 51*
divorci-, > *divorciar, p. 59*
doy, > *dar, p. 64*
duel-, > *doler, p. 52*
duerm-, > *dormir, p. 53*
efectú-/efectu-, > *efectuar, p. 61*
elij-, > *elegir, p. 50, 55*
empiez-, > *empezar, p. 48*
empobrezc-, > *empobrecer, p. 56*
enciend-, > *encender, p. 48*
encuentr-, > *encontrar, p. 52*
enfrí-/enfri-, > *enfriar, p. 60*
engrandezc-, > *engrandecer, p. 56*

engrí-/engri-, > *engreír, p. 50*
enmiend-, > *enmendar, p. 49*
enriquezc-, > *enriquecer, p. 56*
entiend-, > *entender, p. 49*
entierr-, > *enterrar, p. 49*
envejezc-, > *envejecer, p. 56*
enví-/envi-, > *enviar, p. 59*
er-, > *ser, p. 71*
erg-, > *erguir, p. 51, 76*
ergu-, > *erguir, p. 51, 76*
es, > *ser, p. 71*
escarmient-, > *escarmentar, p. 48*
escrit-, > *escribir, p. 74*
esfuerz-, > *esforzarse, p. 52*
esparz-, > *esparcir, p. 56, 76*
espí-/espi-, > *espiar, p. 60*
esquí-/esqui-, > *esquiar, p. 60*
establezc-, > *establecer, p. 56*
estoy, > *estar, p. 65*
estudi-, > *estudiar, p. 59*
estuv-, > *estar, p. 65*
evacú-/evacu-, > *evacuar, p. 60*
evalú-/evalu-, > *evaluar, p. 61*
exceptú-/exceptu-, > *exceptuar, p. 61*
excluy-, > *excluir, p. 58*
extiend-, > *extender, p. 48, 75*
extraví-/extravi-, > *extraviar, p. 60*
fastidi-, > *fastidiar, p. 59*
favorezc-, > *favorecer, p. 56, 75*
fí-/fi-, > *fiar, p. 59*
financi-, > *financiar, p. 59*
finj-, > *fingir, p. 55*
fluctú-/fluctu-, > *fluctuar, p. 61*
fortalezc-, > *fortalecer, p. 56*
fotografí-/fotografi-, > *fotografiar, p. 60*
frí-/fri-, > *freír, p. 50, 74*
frieg-, > *fregar, p. 48*
frit-, > *freír, p. 50, 74*
fu-, > *ir, p. 67, or ser, p. 71*
fuerc-, > *forzar, p. 52, 56*
fuerz-, > *forzar, p. 52, 56*
gim-, > *gemir, p. 50*
gobiern-, > *gobernar, p. 48*
gruñ-, > *gruñir, p. 79*
guí-/gui-, > *guiar, p. 59*
h-, > *haber, p. 65*
habr-, > *haber, p. 65*
hag-, > *hacer, p. 66*
har-, > *hacer, p. 66*
hay, > *haber, p. 7, 15, 36*
haz-, > *hacer, p. 66*
he, > *haber, p. 66*
hech-, > *hacer, p. 66, 74*
hench-, > *henchir, p. 79*
hic-, > *hacer, p. 66*
hiel-, > *helar, p. 48*

85

hier-, > *herir, p. 51*
hierv-, > *hervir, p. 51*
hinch-, > *henchirse, p. 50, 78*
hub-, > *haber, p. 66*
huel-, > *oler, p. 52, 77*
huy-, > *huir, p. 58*
impid-, > *impedir, p. 50*
impres-, > *imprimir, p. 74*
incluy-, > *incluir, p. 58, 75*
influy-, > *influir, p. 58*
inici-, > *iniciar, p. 59*
inquier-, > *inquirir, p. 51, 59*
instituy-, > *instituir, p. 58*
introduj-, > *introducir, p. 57*
introduzc-, > *introducir, p. 57*
inviert-, > *invertir, p. 51*
irg-, > *erguir, p. 76*
irgu-, > *erguir, p. 76*
jueg-, > *jugar, p. 52*
ley-, > *leer, p. 57*
ligu-, > *ligar, p. 54*
llegu-, > *llegar, p. 55*
lluev-, > *llover, p. 52*
luzc-, > *lucir, p. 56*
manifiest-, > *manifestar, p. 48*
mecanografi-/mecanografi-,
   > *mecanografiar, p. 60*
merezc-, > *merecer, p. 56*
meriend-, > *merendar, p. 48*
mez-, > *mecer, p. 56, 76*
mid-, > *medir, p. 50*
mient-, > *mentir, p. 51*
muerd-, > *morder, p. 52*
muert-, > *morir, p. 74*
muestr-, > *mostrar, p. 52*
muev-, > *mover, p. 52*
nazc-, > *nacer, p. 56, 75*
negoci-, > *negociar, p. 59*
nieg-, > *negar, p. 48*
niev-, > *nevar, p. 49*
obedezc-, > *obedecer, p. 56*
obsequi-, > *obsequiar, p. 59*
odi-, > *odiar, p. 59*
ofrezc-, > *ofrecer, p. 56*
oig-, > *oír, p. 67*
oy-, > *oír, p. 67*
padezc-, > *padecer, p. 56*
parezc-, > *parecer, p. 56*
permanezc-, > *permanecer, p. 56*
perpetú-/perpetu-, > *perpetuar, p. 61*
persig-, > *perseguir, p. 50*
pertenezc-, > *pertenecer, p. 56*
pid-, > *pedir, p. 50*
piens-, > *pensar, p. 49*
pierd-, > *perder, p. 49*
podr-, > *poder, p. 68*

pon-, > *poner, p. 69*
pondr-, > *poner, p. 68*
pong-, > *poner, p. 69*
posey-, > *poseer, p. 57*
pres-, > *prender, p. 74*
prevé-, > *prever, p. 77*
prefier-, > *preferir, p. 51*
prevén-, > *prever, p. 77*
prevés-, > *prever, p. 77*
produj-, > *producir, p. 57*
produzc-, > *producir, p. 57*
prohíb-/prohib-, > *prohibir, p. 61*
pronunci-, > *pronunciar, p. 59*
propici-, > *propiciar, p. 59*
prosig-, > *proseguir, p. 50*
protej-, > *proteger, p. 55*
provey-, > *proveer, p. 58*
provist-, > *proveer, p. 58, 74*
prueb-, > *probar, p. 52*
pud-, > *poder, p. 68*
pudr,- > *pudrir, p. 77*
pued-, > *poder, p. 68*
puesto, > *poner, p. 68, 74*
pus-, > *poner, p. 69*
quep-, > *caber, p. 62*
querr-, > *querer, p. 69*
quiebr-, > *quebrar, p. 49*
quier-, > *querer, p. 69*
quis-, > *querer, p. 69*
recomiend-, > *recomendar, p. 49*
reconcili-, > *reconciliar, p. 59*
reconozc-, > *reconocer, p. 56*
recuerd-, > *recordar, p. 52*
reduj-, > *reducir, p. 57*
reduzc-, > *reducir, p. 57*
refier-, > *referirse a, p. 51*
remedi-, > *remediar, p. 59*
renuev-, > *renovar, p. 52*
repit-, > *repetir, p. 50*
requier-, > *requerir, p. 51*
restituy-, > *restituir, p. 58*
resuelt-, > *resolver, p. 75*
reún-/reun-, > *reunir, p. 61*
rí-/ri-, > *reír, p. 50, 77*
rieg-, > *regar, p. 49*
riñ-, > *reñir, p. 50, 78*
rind-, > *rendirse, p. 50*
rot-, > *romper, p. 74*
roy-, > *roer, p. 58*
rueg-, > *rogar, p. 52*
s-, > *ser, p. 71*
sabr-, > *saber, p. 70*
saci-, > *saciar, p. 59*
sal-, > *salir, p. 70*
saldr-, > *salir, p. 70*
salg-, > *salir, p. 70*

86

saqu-, > *sacar, p. 54*
satisfag-, > *satisfacer, p. 56, 79*
satisfar-, > *satisfacer, p. 56, 79*
satisfic-, > *satisfacer, p. 56, 79*
satisfaz-, > *satisfacer, p. 56, 79*
sé, > *ser, p. 71 or saber, p. 69*
sedij-, > *seducir, p. 57*
seduzc-, > *seducir, p. 57*
sep-, > *saber, p. 70*
sieg-, > *segar, p. 49*
siembr-, > *sembrar, p. 49*
sient-, > *sentarse, p. 49*
sient-, > *sentir, p. 51*
sig-, > *seguir, p. 50*
silenci-, > *silenciar, p. 59*
sirv-, > *servir, p. 50*
sitú-/situ-, > *situar, p. 61, 75*
sois, > *ser, p. 71*
somos, > *ser, p. 71*
son, > *ser, p. 71*
sonrí-/sonri-, > *sonreír, p. 50, 77*
soy, > *ser, p. 71*
suel-, > *soler, p. 52*
suelt-, > *soltar, p. 52*
suen-, > *sonar, p. 52*
sueñ-, > *soñar, p. 52*
sup-, > *saber, p. 70*
sustituy-, > *sustituir, p. 58*
taquigrafí-/taquigrafi-,
      > *taquigrafiar, p. 60*
ten-, > *tener, p. 71*
teñ-, > *teñir, p. 50, 75, 79*
teng-, > *tener, p. 71*
tiembl-, > *temblar, p. 49*
tiend-, > *tender, p. 49*
tient-, > *tentar, p. 49*
tiñ-, > *teñir, p. 50, 79*

traduj-, > *traducir, p. 57*
traduzc-, > *traducir, p. 57*
traig-, > *traer, p. 58, 72*
traj-, > *traer, p. 58, 72*
transfier-, > *transferir, p. 51*
trayendo-, > *traer, p. 58*
tropiec-, > *tropezar, p. 49*
tropiez-, > *tropezar, p. 49*
tuerc-, > *torcer, p. 52, 56*
tull-, > *tullir, p. 79*
tuv-, > *tener, p. 71*
v-, > *ir, p. 67*
v-, > *ver, p. 73*
vací-/vaci-, > *vaciar, p. 60*
varí-/vari-, > *variar, p. 60*
vay-, > *ir, p. 67*
ven-, > *venir, p. 72*
veng-, > *venir, p. 72*
venz-, > *vencer, p. 56*
viert-, > *verter, p. 49*
vin-, > *venir, p. 72, 73*
viniendo, > *venir, p. 72*
vist-, > *vestir, p. 50*
visto, > *ver, p. 73, 74*
voy, > *ir, p. 67*
vuel-, > *volar, p. 52*
vuelc-, > *volcar, p. 52*
vuelto, > *volver, p. 74*
vuelv-, > *volver, p. 52*
yag-, > *yacer, p. 47, 56*
yazc-, > *yacer, p. 47, 56*
yazg-, > *yacer, p. 47, 56*
yendo, > *ir, p. 67*
yerg-, > *erguir, p. 51, 76*
yergu-, > *erguir, p. 51, 76*
yerr-, > *errar, p. 77*
zambull-, > *zambullir, p. 79*

Index of Verbs and Prepositions

This Index lists the Prepositions which follow certain common verbs. In some cases they are obligatory, in others they serve to modify the meaning (e.g. **tener** – *to have,* **tener que** – *to have to*). And see p. 32 for the use of personal **a**.

acabar con, *to put an end to*
acabar de, *to have just*
acabar por, *to end up by*
acercarse a, *to approach*
acordarse de, *to remember*
apelar a, *to appeal to*
aprovechar de, *to take advantage of*
aproximarse a, *to approach*
arrimarse a, *to lean against*
asemejarse a, *to resemble*
asomarse a/por, *to lean out of*
asombrarse de, *to be surprised at*
avergonzarse de/por, *to be ashamed of*
cambiar de, *to change*
carecer de, *to lack*
casarse con, *to marry*
compadecerse de, *to feel sorry for*
confinar con, *to border on*
consentir en, *to agree to*
consistir en, *to consist of*
contar con, *to rely on*
contravenir a, *to contravene*
convenir en, *to agree on*
cooperar a, *to cooperate in*
cumplir con, *to fulfil*
decidir de, *to decide*
decidirse a, *to decide*
depender de, *to depend on*
desconfiar de, *to mistrust*
dudar de, *to mistrust*
encargarse de, *to take charge of*
enlazarse en, *to link in with*
entrar en, *to enter*
esforzarse por, *to make an effort*
estar para, *to be about to, to feel like*
estar por, *to be in favour of, to yet be done*
estribar en, *to rest on*
faltar a, *to be lacking in*

felicitar por, *to congratulate on*
fiar en, *to trust, have faith in*
fijarse en, *to notice*
hablar con, *to speak to*
hablar de, *to speak about*
influir en, *to influence*
ingresar en, *to enter*
jugar a, *to play*
lindar con, *to border on*
llamar a, *to appeal to*
maravillarse de, *to wonder at*
mudar de, *to change*
murmurar de, *to criticise*
oler a, *to smell of*
optar por, *to opt for*
parecerse a, *to resemble*
pensar de, *to think of (opinion)*
pensar en, *to think about, to plan*
preguntar por, *to ask after*
prescindir de, *to do without*
reírse de, *to laugh at*
renunciar a, *to give up, renounce*
resistir a, *to resist*
responder de, *to be responsible for*
responsibilizarse por, *to take responsibility for*
saber a, *to taste of*
saber de, *to know about*
semejar a, *to resemble*
sobrevivir a, *to survive*
soñar con, *to dream of*
soñar en, *to think of, plan*
tendar a, *to tend to*
terminar de, *to have just*
terminar por, *to finish up by*
triunfar de, *to triumph over*
variar de, *to change*
vengarse de, *to take revenge*